W9-AAW-558

NOTES

FROM THE

EDGE TIMES

NOTES

FROM THE

EDGE TIMES

DANIEL PINCHBECK

JEREMY P. TARCHER/PENGUIN

a member of Penguin Group (USA) Inc.

New York

JEREMY P. TARCHER/PENGUIN
Published by the Penguin Group
Penguin Group (USA) Inc., 375 Hudson Street, New York, New York
10014, USA • Penguin Group (Canada), 90 Eglinton Avenue East,
Suite 700, Toronto, Ontario M4P 2Y3, Canada (a division of Pearson Penguin Canada
Inc.) • Penguin Books Ltd, 80 Strand, London WC2R 0RL, England • Penguin
Ireland, 25 St Stephen's Green, Dublin 2, Ireland (a division of Penguin Books
Ltd) • Penguin Group (Australia), 250 Camberwell Road, Camberwell, Victoria 3124,
Australia (a division of Pearson Australia Group Pty Ltd) • Penguin Books India Pvt
Ltd, 11 Community Centre, Panchsheel Park, New Delhi–110 017, India • Penguin
Group (NZ), 67 Apollo Drive, Rosedale, North Shore 0632, New Zealand (a division
of Pearson New Zealand Ltd) • Penguin Books (South Africa) (Pty) Ltd,
24 Sturdee Avenue, Rosebank, Johannesburg 2196, South Africa

Penguin Books Ltd, Registered Offices: 80 Strand, London WC2R 0RL, England

Most Tarcher/Penguin books are available at special quantity discounts for bulk
purchase for sales promotions, premiums, fund-raising, and educational needs. Special
books or book excerpts also can be created to fit specific needs. For details, write
Penguin Group (USA) Inc. Special Markets, 375 Hudson Street, New York, NY 10014.

Library of Congress Cataloging-in-Publication Data

Pinchbeck, Daniel.
Notes from the edge times / Daniel Pinchbeck.
p.   cm.
ISBN 978-1-58542-837-3
1. Prophecies (Occultism).   2. Consciousness.   3. Mayas—Prophecies.
4. Twenty-first century—Forecasts.   5. Spiritual life—New Age movement.   I. Title.
BF1791.P56   2010   2010023995
001.9—dc22

Printed in the United States of America
1   3   5   7   9   10   8   6   4   2

BOOK DESIGN BY NICOLE LAROCHE

For my mother, Joyce Johnson

CONTENTS

INTRODUCTION: AFTER THE DISASTER   *1*

THE OPEN HAND   *11*

FROM EGO TO WE GO   *15*

MISSION POSSIBLE   *19*

THE GNOSTIC REVIVAL   *23*

OUR FORGOTTEN FUTURE   *27*

MEETING THE SPIRITS   *31*

THE SEXUAL REVOLUTION, TAKE TWO   *35*

LIFE DURING WARTIME   *39*

THE ALMIGHTY AMERO   *43*

"2012" AND THE POET'S DILEMMA   *47*

BLACKWATER RUNS DEEP   54

ALIEN NATION   58

MILITARY MINDFIELDS   62

YOUR MONEY AND YOUR LIFE   66

OLD STRUGGLES ON A NEW EARTH   70

THE END OF MONEY?   74

ENLIGHTENMENT REASON
OR OCCULT CONSPIRACY?   85

THE FUTURE OF PSYCHEDELICS   89

NONVIOLENT ACTION
AS SPIRITUAL PRACTICE   94

2008: THE RETURN OF CHICKEN LITTLE   99

IF I WERE PRESIDENT . . .   103

ABSORBING ORBS   107

TRANSITION TOWN   111

PUT A FORK IN IT (THE GLOBAL
FINANCIAL SYSTEM IS DONE)   *115*

BREAKDOWN AND BREAKTHROUGH   *120*

THE PRESENT OF PRESENCE   *124*

THE INTENTION ECONOMY   *128*

THE AGE OF UNCERTAINTY   *132*

AN EXTRAVAGANT HYPOTHESIS   *136*

BUILDING A SCAFFOLD
FOR SOCIAL CHANGE   *140*

SATELLITE OF LOVE: THOUGHTS
ON THE NORWAY SPIRAL   *144*

MY JOURNEY INTO THE EVOLVER
SOCIAL MOVEMENT   *154*

AFTERWORD: THE NEED TO BELIEVE   *171*

Special Thanks   *194*
About the Author   *195*

Recently, a $250 million film linked the year 2012 with a mass wipeout of humanity from earth crust displacement and super-volcano spew. The spectacle seemed designed to curtail any deeper thought or discussion of the subject by making it appear ridiculous. Apparently, I was parodied in the film, as *The New York Times* noted: "Though not much is made of the Mayan angle, the most amusing character, a doomsday prophet and radio broadcaster played by Woody Harrelson, seems in hair, beard and interests to have been drawn along the predictive lines of the real author Daniel Pinchbeck."

Although my ideas run counter to what the filmmakers proposed, I allowed myself to be incorporated into their marketing and promotion machinery. I was invited by Sony Pictures to be one of three "2012 experts," along with authors Lawrence E. Joseph and John Major Jenkins. The three of us were flown to Jackson Hole, Wyoming, where we were given the chance to address the global media during a press junket, and then to Los Angeles for the appropriately black-carpeted premiere. While I had reservations, I accepted the offers because I hoped to use the opportunity to convey a different message. As the media reduced my ideas to sound bites or hopelessly distorted them, I felt as if a mask of cultural fears and misconceptions was projected onto my face. This was not surprising, but it was still unsettling.

In *2012: The Return of Quetzalcoatl,* my previous book, I described, as truthfully as I could, my exploration of subjects including psychedelic shamanism, the crop circle phenomenon in the UK, and indigenous prophecies. While a number of visionaries, systems theorists, and a few whack jobs propose that something radical, absolutely astonishing, and unprecedented is going to happen as we pass through the 2012 portal—galactic synchronization, mass DMT activation, sudden ascension, huge solar storm, galactic superwave—I never predicted a definitive outcome. Our culture imposes a dualistic divide between the psychic and physical aspects of our world. I believe we are learning that this split is untenable. History is also myth, and science is also story. If we are on the verge of a radical change, part of that transmutation will be a shift in perspective, from the flat, literalized worldview of our modern scientific and material culture to a new paradigm that reconciles the psychic and imaginal dimensions with what we believe to be purely physical aspects of our existence.

The hypothesis that the year 2012 signifies the end of a cycle is derived from the extraordinary civilization of the Classical Maya. From the second century A.D., the Maya developed an advanced, highly stratified civilization, ruled by wizard-kings, that extended across the Yucatán Peninsula of Mexico, through Guatemala and Honduras. Perhaps because of ecological overreach or for other unknown reasons, the Maya abandoned most of their temple complexes and stone cities quite suddenly, around the tenth century A.D. Millions of indigenous Maya continue to live in these lands today, following their traditional ways.

The achievements of this culture included a highly developed mathematics, precise astronomical tabulations, incredible art, and an advanced calendar system. While the indigenous Maya still keep a sacred calendar of 260 days, the Classical Maya also followed a Long Count calendar of over five thousand years that ends on the winter solstice of 2012. There is little surviving evidence that the Maya believed any particular event would occur on that precise date. The culture of the Classical Maya centered on ritualized, shamanic practices used to attain non-ordinary states of consciousness and gain visionary knowledge. Since modern civilization rejected these practices and techniques, it is extremely difficult, if not impossible, for us to access their mind-set and their approach to knowledge.

Esteemed Mayan archaeologists, such as Michael Coe of Yale University, agree that the Classical Maya saw the end of their Long Count calendar to be the hinge of a shift between "World Ages." In the Popol Vuh, the Mayan creation myth, these world ages end with the demolition of humanity in its current state, and its re-creation in a different, perhaps more evolved, form. Despite hints from the Popol Vuh, nobody knows what the Classical Maya expected to happen as we pass from one world age to the next.

Following the work of Terence McKenna, researcher John Major Jenkins put forth the thesis that the Maya correlated the end of the Long Count with a rare astronomical alignment, in which the winter solstice sun eclipses the dark rift at the center of the Milky Way. The Maya may have chosen to focus on this alignment because it positions us in relationship to the surrounding galaxy. There is no known causal reason why such an astronomical event—essentially, an optical alignment only meaningful from our earthly perspective—would have any tangible effect on the physical world. Whether the timeframe is prophetically aligned or purely accidental, some contemporary astrophysicists fret that a sudden increase in solar activity could shut down the electrical grid on or around 2012; at the same time, a number of gloomy economists forecast a global financial meltdown in the next few years.

Despite all of the question marks around the subject, "2012" provides a focusing lens and an opportunity to rethink the direction of our current civilization. Instead of fixating on any particular date, we should appreciate that any positive transformation, whether in 2012 or after, will only be the result of deliberate actions and conscious choices made by human beings, here and now. Despite the intensifying evolutionary pressures we face and the telescoped timeframe in which progress and change now occur, we remain a half-awake, half-conscious species. As individuals, we tend to be vain, fragile, self-serving, ego-centered. The organizations and institutions we create reflect our individual flaws.

Notes from the Edge Times presents, in chronological order, essays I published over the last few years, since the release of *2012: The Return of Quetzalcoatl.* A few of these pieces first appeared in my Web magazine, *Reality Sandwich*, and many of them ran in *Conscious Choice*, which was for a few years a consortium of four magazines on health and alternative spirituality, published in Chicago, Seattle, Los Angeles, and San Francisco. In my columns, I offered my ever-changing perspective on the ongoing process of social change and consciousness evolution. These pieces also chronicle my personal struggle to move from contemplation of our situation to direct action to make change.

This much seems inarguable: We find ourselves in a window of opportunity where we either radically alter our direction as a species or face devastating consequences. We are at that threshold where, as the social ecologist Murray Bookchin put it in *The Ecology of Freedom*, our world "will either undergo revolutionary changes, so far-reaching in character that humanity will totally transform its social relations and its very conception of life, or it will suffer an apocalypse that may well end humanity's tenure on the planet." Examining accelerating trends in climate change and species extinction, the scientist James Lovelock, who is often credited with developing the Gaia Hypothesis, thinks that only 150 million people will be left alive at the end of this century. Other scientists share his ominous outlook. As resources such as fuel and fresh water become scarce, it is quite likely we will see more horrific wars, masses of refugees, famines, droughts, pandemics, and revolutions.

If the outlook from a purely empirical perspective looks bleak, the good news is that science has ignored some crucial factors. One is the possibility that human beings, through a rapid evolution of consciousness, could develop a regenerative culture that contributes to the health of the biosphere. In the 1960s, the design scientist Buckminster Fuller proposed that society could be redesigned to be "comprehensively successful" for everyone on earth. In the short term, we could become far more flexible and resilient, re-localizing the production of basic essentials, such as food, energy, clothes, and shelter, while liberating knowledge as a free resource and commonwealth. We could institute "cradle to cradle" manufacturing practices to protect the environment, and use the techniques of nonviolent protest developed by Gandhi to stop the spread of GMOs and end unjust wars. We could supplant the current form of money, as an exclusive measure of value controlled by private banking interests, with a number of new systems for exchanging goods and services that support collaboration and trust over competition and self-interest. Despite geopolitical gridlock, we have the tools we need to restore the natural systems we have corrupted and create a new planetary culture based on mutual aid and equitable sharing of resources.

Another factor ignored by science and the mainstream is the validity of paranormal phenomena, psychic capabilities, or what Carl Jung called "the reality of the Psyche." There is much evidence supporting the existence of psychic abilities, and many people experience such phenomena regularly. As an analogy, we can consider the recent discovery and application of electricity. Once engineers learned how to conduct and store electricity in the nineteenth century, we transformed the entire earth in less than two centuries, a blink of evolutionary time. If we can discover reliable means to access, utilize, and channel psychic energy, we might participate in yet another rapid transformation of our world. Visionary thinker José Argüelles proposes that our future culture will be "psycho-technic:" We will apply our modern technical acuity to the exploration of those hidden dimensions of psychic experience and extrasensory perception that modern society suppressed during this recent phase of material and technological progress.

The chance for a conscious and participatory social evolution is predicated on a great awakening happening quickly—before ecological meltdown leads to systemic breakdown. People have the opportunity to attain self-knowledge, to discover the depth dimensions of psychic life rejected by modern society. They can anchor these realizations in their daily lives and habits. Spiritual illumination is only meaningful when it is integrated through social commitment and courageous action. Since post-industrial civilization currently threatens the natural functions of the biosphere, escaping the effects of our culture is no longer possible. Whether we like it or not, each one of us is a social and political agent whose actions influence many other people and impact the larger world around us. Our current culture extols irresponsibility, greed, and waste. If humanity chooses to awaken to its potential and confront the crisis we have unleashed, the culture that supersedes this one will express different values and run on a radically revamped operating system.

While it is conceivable that 2012 may see some sudden quantum shift in human consciousness or an alien landing on the White House lawn, it is likely that we have a much longer struggle ahead of us. In that case, the end of the Long Count will still be significant as the hinge of a transition in our species' awareness. An ever-growing subset of the population is becoming aware of the archaic mind-set of domination and blinkered rationalism that degrades the environment, wipes out traditional cultures, and keeps the masses locked in a prison of constricted awareness. As more and more of us realize this, we will find each other and collaborate, overcoming the inertia of the old system as we design and develop new ways to live—not just on but with the earth.

We find ourselves in a time of immense pressure and dazzling opportunity. As we crack nature's codes, humanity could become a star-faring species, conquer disease and even death through biotechnology, develop immersive virtual worlds out of silicon bits, or quickly fail and become extinct. Alternatively, we could regain, through what psychedelic philosopher Terence McKenna called an "archaic revival," aspects of our aboriginal past, restoring dormant psychic capacities and making a new sacred pact with the cosmos. However it all goes down, I consider this the most inspiring moment to be alive in the history of our species. I feel exceedingly lucky as well as grateful for this ongoing opportunity to learn from and reflect upon it. I hope you will enjoy these modest excursions—explorations into the edge-realms, forays into the perils and potentials of our time—and that you will discover something in them that inspires you, fires your imagination, and takes you on a few new twists and turns down the slippery slopes of our shared reality tunnel.

—DANIEL PINCHBECK
Spring 2010

THE OPEN HAND

Traditionally, writers have the job of defining the zeitgeist, but that task has never been as difficult as it is today. While this seems a singular and remarkable moment in human history, there is something indefinable about it. The weather is certainly strange—I live in New York City, where temperatures in early January remain about fifteen degrees above normal, and spring flowers started to bloom before Christmas. The political situation is most definitely peculiar—our military engages in a senseless campaign that has lasted longer than World War II, with hundreds of billions of dollars spent on spreading death and misery. We read about icebergs breaking up and a frightening lack of fish in the seas, yet there is plenty of ice for our drinks, and caviar is making a comeback.

We swim in new psychic waters. We may understand, to a greater or lesser degree, that global civilization has hit the resource limits of the biosphere, but such a general foreboding is useless. We can recycle lightbulbs or build a green roof. These gestures are meaningful, but they seem almost farcical compared to the magnitude of the problem.

The contradictions between our intentions and our actions are almost head-splitting.

My perspective is that we are experiencing an accelerated evolution of human consciousness. Right now, we find ourselves in an awkward transition between steadier states. For the last centuries, a limited form of scientific rationality ruled the modern world, a mind-set that denied intuitive thought and saw nature as an enemy to be conquered. We developed technologies that embodied our sense of alienation and isolation. Many of us are now reaching a different perspective. As we make connections between quantum physics and Eastern mysticism, we realize we live in a participatory universe, with no place for an objective observer. Intuition is not irrational, but arational—it is the way our mind processes the overload of information that doesn't enter our conscious filter.

My own quest for understanding led me from being a somewhat embittered New York journalist to hitting a massive spiritual crisis in the late 1990s. In the throes of existential despair, I remembered my psychedelic experiences from college, and decided to pursue the subject as a journalist. I took an assignment to undergo a tribal initiation in Gabon, in West Africa, where I ate a visionary rootbark, iboga (also known as ibogaine). I traveled to the Amazon in Ecuador to drink ayahuasca—a hallucinatory potion—with the Secoya Indians, and visited the Mazatecs in Mexico, who preserve a sacred culture using mushrooms.

The results of these investigations, and more, are recorded in my first book, *Breaking Open the Head*, which described my shift over time from cynical materialism to an acceptance of other dimensions and occult aspects of the psyche. By the end, I had plunged into Carl Jung, Rudolf Steiner, Walter Benjamin, Carlos Castaneda, and many more, in an attempt to figure out what was going on. For my second book, *2012: The Return of Quetzalcoatl*, I investigated the nature of prophecy, particularly the sacred calendar kept by the Classical Maya in the Yucatán, which completes a "Great Cycle" of more than five thousand years in the year 2012. Most modern people find it far-fetched that a non-technological and myth-based civilization, such as the Maya, might have developed a different system of knowledge that is more advanced than our own, in certain respects. In *2012*, I conclude that this is possible.

Somehow, from over a thousand years ago, the Maya predicted that this time would be crucial for humanity—and, indeed, it is. In the next few years, I believe that we are either going to slide into chaos, or institute a new planetary culture based on compassion and rational use of resources. The second option requires a quantum leap in consciousness—but, as I argued in *2012*, our entire history has prepared us for that leap, when we view it from a certain perspective.

It has been exactly forty years since the heyday of the 1960s. That epoch could be viewed as an attempted voyage of initiation for the modern world. Today, we have embarked upon a new phase of the initiatory journey begun a generation ago—with the opportunity to avoid the tactical mistakes, strident statements, and polarizations of the past. Increasing numbers of people pursue spiritual practices, such as yoga and shamanism, with disciplined intensity. Perhaps, with an inchoate sense of foreknowledge, many people are preparing themselves for the transformation just ahead.

As our civilization races heedlessly toward ecological cataclysm, we have also reached a point where the old separations between political parties, identity groups, and classes are no longer serving us and have become counterproductive. Artificial divisions can be superseded to create a new unified initiative. Those who have developed a deeper understanding of our current situation, and a wider perspective on what type of positive transformation might occur, should, naturally, be the ones who reach out toward people still trapped in fear, greed, and paranoia. If some elements of the 1960s are returning, they are doing so without the oppositional anger of the past. The open hand, offering friendship and reconciliation, has replaced the raised-fist symbol of old-style activism.

When I was in my twenties, literature was my ruling passion, and my heroes were writers like Fitzgerald, Kerouac, Virginia Woolf, and Henry Miller. I longed to emulate the passionate intensity of their prose, and the "negative capability" that infused their characters with recognizable life. When I passed through the crucible of my own transformational process, I lost interest in novels and discovered a new pantheon of intellectual heroes. These days, I find the same level of electrical engagement that I used to find in novels in the works of thinkers whose central theme is the evolution and possible extension of human consciousness. This varied group is made up of mystics, physicists, philosophers, cosmologists, and paleontologists—the roster includes Rudolf Steiner, Carl Jung, Edward Edinger, Jean Gebser, Pierre Teilhard de Chardin, F. David Peat, Sri Aurobindo, and Gerald Heard.

For me personally, most contemporary fiction, like most current film, has an increasingly retrograde quality. In their efforts to make their audience identify with a particular drama or trauma or relationship saga, these products seem almost nostalgic. We live in a culture that continually seeks to entertain or at least distract us with an endless spew of personal narratives, whether paraded on lowbrow talk shows or parsed in literary novels. If you step outside of the cultural framing, you suddenly become aware of the mechanism that keeps us addicted to the spectacle—and, above all, hooked on ego. Our entire culture is dedicated to inciting and then placating the desires and fears of the individual ego—what the media critic Thomas de Zengotita calls "the flattered self."

Although they use different language to define it, the various theorists on the evolution of the psyche all agree that the crux of our current crisis requires that we transcend the ego. They suggest that the stage of material progress and scientific discovery we attained in recent centuries is not the end of human development, but the launching pad for another stage in our growth. However, this next stage differs from previous phases in one essential way—it requires a "mutation in consciousness" that can only be self-willed and self-directed. According to this paradigm, it is as if physical evolution has done billions of years of work on our behalf, to get us to this point. Right now, it is our choice whether we would like to go forward, or fall by the wayside like untold millions of other species, who over-adapted to one set of conditions, and could not re-create themselves as their environment changed.

In his influential book *Pain, Sex and Time*, the British polymath Gerald Heard defined three stages in human evolution—physical, technical, and psychical. "The first is unconscious—blind; the second is conscious, unreflective, aware of its need but not of itself, of how, not why; the third is interconscious, reflective, knowing not merely how to satisfy its needs but what they mean and the Whole means," wrote Heard, who believed we were on the cusp of switching from the technical to the psychical level of development. As we enter the psychic phase, we shift "from indirect to direct expansion of understanding, at this point man's own self-consciousness decides and can alone decide whether he will mutate, and the mutation is instantaneous." Originally published in 1939, Heard's book has just been reprinted in the United States; it was James Dean's favorite work, and inspired Huston Smith to turn to religious studies.

Despite its antique provenance, *Pain, Sex and Time* remains "new news" for our time. Heard viewed the immense capacity of human beings to experience pain and suffering, and the extraordinary excess of our sexual drive compared to our actual reproductive needs, as signs of a tremendous surplus of evolutionary energy that can be repurposed for the extension and intensification of consciousness, if we so choose. "Modern man's incessant sexuality is not bestial: rather it is a psychic hemorrhage," Heard wrote. "He bleeds himself constantly because he fears mental apoplexy if he can find no way of releasing his huge store of nervous energy." Heard foresaw the necessity of a new form of self-discipline, a training in concentrating psychic energy to develop extrasensory perception, as the proper way to channel the excess of nervous hypertension that would otherwise lead to our destruction. He thought that we would either evolve into a "supraindividual" condition, or the uncontrolled energies would force us back into "preindividuated" identifications, leading to nationalist wars and totalitarian fervors, and species burnout.

A sign I saw at last year's Burning Man put it succinctly: "From Ego to We Go." As the climate changes and our environment deteriorates, we are being subjected to tremendous evolutionary pressures that could push us beyond individuation, into a deeply collaborative mind-set and a new threshold of psychic awareness. Seventy years after Heard's manifesto, whether or not we want to evolve as a species remains an open question. But the choice is in our hands.

MISSION POSSIBLE

When people in our culture want to be enthralled and inspired by a story, we run to the movies, where dramas of life, death, and redemption are played out at pulse-pounding high speed. Most of us do not fully realize that we are currently participating in a real-life thriller that could go as down-to-the-wire as any episode of *Mission Impossible* or *Star Wars*. The crux of this plot line is whether global humanity can awaken from its current trance—our fixation on materialist progress and economic growth—in time to salvage the biosphere, and our own future.

According to current calculations, 25 percent of all mammalian species—potentially all species in general—will be extinct within thirty years, at present rates. All tropical forests will disappear within forty years, as all ocean fisheries collapse within the same timeframe. As climate change accelerates, it is creating unpredictable feedback loops, potentially leading to global food shortages as droughts and deluges affect agricultural tables. Mass species extinction could also cause feedback loops that would make life on earth untenable for large mammals such as ourselves. The large-scale disappearance of amphibians, butterflies, and

honeybees in recent decades seems an unambiguous warn-
ing signal.

Confronted with the frightening evidence of planetary
decimation, many of us prefer to flinch away and retreat
into our private concerns. We have to find the courage to
overcome this tendency. Instead of inciting pessimism or
fatalism, the dire predictions can compel us to deepen our
commitment to transformation. If a few decades are all
that separate us from cataclysm, then the "ecological U-turn"
in global consciousness must be accomplished in the next
few years.

One way that massive change could happen quickly is
through a paradigm shift in the mainstream media. While
the United States has lost much of its standing in the world
in recent years, we still operate the controls of the collective dream-machinery for the planet. The blueprint for a
better life now being pursued by the masses and entrepre-
neurial classes across Asia, India, and the Third World is
the "American Dream" of unlimited affluence, promoted
by our television shows and films over the last half-century.
A transformation of values—a spiritual revolution—in
the United States could initiate a global shift in priorities.
If we used our genius for marketing and storytelling to
project a different vision and value system, we could repattern and reprogram the collective psyche in a very short
period of time.

This new media paradigm would encourage participation over passivity, collaboration over individual success,

attunement to local differences over acquiescence to mass marketing, and sufficiency over abundance. The "new news" would focus on trends that support sustainability and higher consciousness, and relentlessly expose techniques of fear-mongering, social control, and "greenwashing." Rather than exploiting violence and sex to grab at the public's fleeting attention, our media would present strategies of conflict resolution and nonviolent practices, while offering a positive revisioning of eroticism as a tool for personal growth.

Responding to the necessity of the planetary crisis, the reinvented mass media would promote the attainment of happiness through nonmaterial means. Such a proposition may seem unrealistic—but at a time when our future as a species is imperiled, we might want to reconsider our concept of "realism." A drastic change in media messaging to align with the real needs of people and planet is preferable to system crash and biospheric meltdown. Corporate decision-makers are also parents and grandparents, who presumably want to see the world continue for their descendants.

We can also change the old paradigm through the accelerated development of new media channels and interactive formats on the Internet. Historically, when a major new media technology emerges, it leads to profound changes in the social system. Just as mass democracy was made possible by the Gutenberg printing press, a new politics with new organizing principles may arise out of the instantaneous interactivity and reputation systems of the Internet.

We are reaching that point where, as the social ecologist Murray Bookchin put it, our world "will either undergo revolutionary changes, so far-reaching in character that humanity will totally transform its social relations and its very conception of life, or it will suffer an apocalypse that may well end humanity's tenure on the planet." Despite the system's inertia, we have the capacity to restore the natural systems we have corrupted, and create a new planetary culture based on communality of interest.

In my head, I keep writing my own movie or reality TV show of the next few years. In this gripping adventure yarn, the ticking time bomb of ignorance and greed gets defused at the last moment by teams of stylish secret agents of consciousness and compassion, working in coordination across the planet. These Tantric technicians create wilderness corridors for endangered species, end sectarian conflicts among warring factions, deploy alternative technologies at appropriate scales, and generally transmute negative vibes to harmonic frequencies. Our current world-movie appears to be moving toward a major showdown. As the virtuosic director of this spectacle, God (or Brahma, or the archetypal Self, or whatever name you care to use) is sure to produce some great and unexpected plot twists in the final reels.

THE GNOSTIC REVIVAL

I first encountered the work of John Lamb Lash through his Web site, metahistory.org, when he posted a series of pieces on "2012"—the end of the Long Count of the Mayan Calendar—from astrological and historical perspectives. In his essays, he defined the characteristics of various "end-time tribes" that were embodying aspects of futuristic consciousness. I began a dialogue with him on this subject, and he sent me his new book, *Not in His Image: Gnostic Vision, Sacred Ecology, and the Future of Belief.* This work is a tremendous achievement that reframes the debate about monotheism, offering a radical perspective on the destructive effects that have been unleashed by religious ideologies over the last two millennia.

Not in His Image attacks the salvationist theology of the Judeo-Christian tradition from a Gnostic perspective, making a devastating critique of the moral conditioning and deep-buried suppositions of this heritage, which has shaped the modern Western psyche. As substitute, Lash presents a countermyth and alternative cosmology drawn from the tradition of Gnosticism, featuring the goddess Sophia, who plunged from the Pleroma to become the physical and generative Earth, and the Archons, soulless off-planet entities who use the human propensity for error to lead us into increasingly destructive deviations from our evolutionary path.

The populist and academic conception of Gnosticism considers it a radical offshoot from Christianity that was stamped out as the Holy Roman Empire gave way to the Dark Ages. Lash has a different perspective. In his view, the Gnostics were the inheritors of the wisdom and initiatory training of the Mystery Schools that flourished across the Classical World. This learned, pagan tradition had roots in the shamanic practices that predated the rise of Greece and Rome, and could be considered the indigenous spirituality of Europe. In some respects similar to Buddhism, the Gnostic tradition valued philosophical debate and direct mystical experience over received wisdom and authority vested in religious hierarchy. Lash connects Sophia to the modern "Gaia hypothesis," developed by the scientists James Lovelock and Lynn Margulis, and argues that the Gnostic seers of the Mystery Schools were "deep ecologists" who taught "coevolution with Gaia." The alienation from the natural world and the body that developed in Christianity was the result of a deception, leading to the "enslavement of humanity to an alien, off-planet agenda." The Gnostics understood the basis of this error, and were persecuted for voicing their opposition to it.

Lash is ruthless in analyzing the moral precepts and core concepts of the Old and New Testament. He shows the ways in which these texts were designed to appeal to the highest aspirations and ideals of humanity, but subtly twisted to create impossible incongruities. Humans were tricked into trying to conform to an inhuman code of perfection, which doomed them to continual failure in relation to an absolutist abstraction. Borrowing a concept from Tibetan Buddhism, Lash suggests substituting the concept of "basic goodness" for "original sin," and argues that Gnostics were horrified by the Christian belief in the redemptive value of suffering.

He argues that the moral ethos expressed by Jesus Christ—the "Divine Victim"—in the New Testament has the unfortunate effect of aiding what he calls our "victim/ perpetrator" bond. The concept of "turning the other cheek," for instance, only makes sense in a world without aggressors. This precept instills a sense of otherworldly superiority in the victims of violence, while it helps the agenda of those who seek to dominate. "The ethic of cheek turning is utterly wrong because it obliges people who are not inclined to harm others to rely on those who do harm to embrace the same practice of nondefense."

The commandment to "love thy God with all thy heart" is similarly distorted: "Who really needs to be commanded to love?" Lash asks. "We love spontaneously, through the power of love itself, which cannot be commanded." Throughout the Gospels, Lash finds "a monumental effort to convert the human mind to the bad faith of betrayed humanity." In our secular culture, it seems, the belief in a salvationist power that will liberate humanity at some future point has been transferred, unconsciously, from divinity to technology. In order to reconnect with our earthly powers, we have to de-program ourselves from all concepts of a redemptive or divine force waiting outside of this realm.

While Lash evinces a tendency to romanticize traditional and indigenous cultures, while ignoring some of the progress made by modern civilization, his critique still goes to the heart of the crisis of our current world, where disconnection from nature and entrenched belief systems have brought us to the brink of global chaos. It seems that we can't find our way forward until we find our way back, utilizing that discriminatory intelligence—what the Gnostics called "nous"—that is our particular human gift.

The future is not what it used to be. What does our future look like from this particular point in time? Scanning the distressing ecological data, we might find ourselves reminded of Marlene Dietrich's exit line to Orson Welles in *Touch of Evil*: "Your future's all used up." From the Oscar-nominated *Children of Men* to Cormac McCarthy's novel *The Road*, recent portraits of what may be coming down the pike have distinctly faded to black—sterile, war-torn wastelands where huddled masses forage for survival. These visions reflect the images we see from today's Iraq, Afghanistan, and Darfur. They suggest a darkening of the collective psyche, a reduced capacity to envision a way out from the encroaching crises that we intuit but lack the will or courage to confront. Novels and films of apocalypse function as avoidance mechanisms, allowing us to imagine global doom from a comfortably alienated vantage point.

As the mainstream absorbs no-exit narratives of breakdowns ahead, the New Age and spiritual set have seized upon an almost antithetical attitude of naive positivity, reflected in wildly popular works like *What the Bleep Do We Know!?* and *The Secret*. From this perspective, the individual's psychic state determines his or her physical reality, and the occult laws of attraction can be utilized to increase one's bank account or sexual magnetism. If you haven't cashed out, it is because you are not using your psychic powers at their maximum rate. If other people aren't getting theirs yet, it's not your problem, but their bad karma. This is a metaphysics suited to the narcissism of the baby boomers and the "Me Generation," whose lifestyles have denuded the planet's rain forests and ripped big holes in the ozone layer.

What makes this perspective so seductive is that there are fragments of truth in it. In my own life and the lives of many people I know, the power of intention is becoming more evident. Reality seems increasingly psychic, as we relearn, step by step, the lessons of synchronicity and nonduality well known to tribal shamans and realized mystics. However, as we access what Carl Jung called "the reality of the psyche," we also discover the huge gap between the small-time desires of the ego and the deeper purposes of the Self, our complete personality, encompassing conscious and unconscious elements. The Self doesn't give a hoot if we drive a fancy car or score with supermodels, and might even prefer to smash the delusions of the ego to incite a deeper realization.

Although I published a book on indigenous prophecy and the year 2012, which ends the 5,125-year Long Count of the Maya, my thoughts on the future continue to fluctuate (as Ralph Waldo Emerson noted, "A foolish consistency is the hobgoblin of little minds"). Between the various camps of technological utopians (see Ray Kurzweil's *The Singularity Is Near*), ecological pessimists, left-wing conspiracists, rapture-ready fundamentalists, and New Age fantasists, one can experience schizo delirium. Is it possible that sudden crisis, such as coastal flooding or nuclear terrorism, will lead to a system meltdown that will change everything? Is it conceivable that most of the world will continue to disintegrate as wealthy First Worlders get stem cell injections, new DNA, and nanobot implants? Or perhaps a rapid shift in global consciousness will lead to a new compassionate planetary culture, with shared resources and technologies based on nontoxic processes and biomimicry? In any event, unless the Law of Attraction can overcome the basic laws of physics, a contraction of industrial civilization seems inevitable.

The trickster element undermining all future predictions is the reality of the psyche, and the possibility that psychic energy could be harnessed for purposes of planetary transformation. If we look back at the Industrial Revolution, before the eighteenth century, people had experienced lightning and shocks, but nobody had any idea how to make use of electricity. Once we figured this out, we changed the geophysical conditions of the planet in a century and a half—not even a blink in evolutionary time. What if we are hovering on the brink of learning how to access and make use of psychic energy in a similar way? If this were the case, it would require a different approach from the modern scientific method that allows no place for subjectivity. Psychic effects cannot be separated from the subjective states that do not so much produce as induce them. If we want to create the conditions in which psychic energy and intention can influence the material world in a reliable and measurable way, we will have to develop a deep sensitivity to unquantifiable aspects of human experience such as mood, atmosphere, and emotion.

Considering this, it is possible that works like *The Secret* and *What the Bleep* have real importance. They could be transitional expressions, pointing us toward a new paradigm of psychic energy and intention that will become more sophisticated as it develops. It seems likely that the current interlocked problems facing our world simply cannot be solved by rational means—but they could be dissolved, if they are approached from a different level of consciousness, and a deeper realization of the psyche.

MEETING THE SPIRITS

All through my childhood, I felt certain that something extraordinary—absolutely amazing and out of the ordinary—was going to happen to me. The world seemed bursting with a secret that nobody would divulge, and someday this tremendous mystery would be revealed. Simply because they were older, I assumed that all adults had passed through this portal into the miraculous essence of existence, although they never spoke about it. As I approached adolescence, I began to suspect that my deepest hopes were going to be unfulfilled. By the time I went to college, I had realized, to my horror, that "maturity" meant accepting constraints and being bound to a limited career path, rather than blossoming into a deeper dimension of possibility and wonder. This was a painful shock.

I now suspect that what I felt is a nearly universal disappointment for young people in our world: I was yearning for initiation in a culture that had abandoned it. Initiatory techniques and rituals have been an essential part of human cultures for tens of thousands of years. In tribal and aboriginal societies, initiations serve a number of different purposes. On one level, rites of passage create a threshold between childhood and adulthood, marking a major life boundary. They are also a time when the elders pass on oral traditions and knowledge to the young. But most important, the traditional process of initiation involves a disciplined training in extrasensory perception and non-ordinary states of consciousness—learning to communicate with the spirit worlds that lie beyond the limits of our physical senses.

While our modern secular culture denies the existence of a spiritual dimension to life, many of our popular post-secular movements of mysticism still refuse to address the question of spirits. Philosophers such as Ken Wilber tend to reduce them to psychological tropes or delusions. Based on my own experiences, I strongly suspect we need to attain a more sophisticated understanding of how spirits may operate, as well as a set of techniques for dealing with them, before we can attain higher states and stages of development. We cannot have "Spirit" without spirits, just as we can't have bodies without the cells and molecules of which they are composed.

For many indigenous cultures, it is a high priority to stay on good terms with the ancestor spirits, who can wreak havoc if they are not given respect. The living and the dead maintain a reciprocal relationship. For the indigenous Maya, if the dead are not handled properly, their ghosts hang around, inflicting neuroses, addictive patterns, and depressions upon their descendants. Such a perspective does not conflict with modern psychology, but adds a deeper dimension to it. As Amit Goswami explores in *The Self-Aware Universe*, quantum physics offers the possibility that incorporeal patterns of thinking, feeling, and action might continue and have effects in the world, even without a physical reference point in a living organism.

One way we could consider our current situation in the United States, perhaps, is as a case of spirit possession on a mass scale. Since we dismiss spirits as nonexistent, we have no defenses against the forces that prey upon us. When a college student guns down his classmates, when a soldier tortures a defenseless victim, when corporate officers avoid facing the environmental consequences of their profit-making, we might be looking at situations in which unappeased demons and aggrieved ancestor spirits are overtaking people, entering their psyches in states of detachment and disconnection. Such a situation cannot be solved through rational means alone, but calls for shamanic techniques such as soul retrieval and banishment.

Personally, my youthful sense of being cheated of some deeper potential melted away once I discovered shamanic practices as an adult, and explored visionary states of consciousness in traditional ceremonies in South America, West Africa, and the United States. Through this work, I restored the primordial connection to the sacred that I had lost after my childhood, as well as my original sense of wonder, and this was tremendously healing and empowering. Through my own shamanic journeys, I realized that modern culture was facing an initiatory crisis on a global scale. We have created a planet of "kidults," perpetual adolescents trapped by material desires, with no access to higher realms and little sense of purpose or moral responsibility.

Despite the best efforts of people like Robert Bly and Malidoma Somé, we are not going to institute a new culture of initiation in the next few years. As Westerners, each of us has to follow a personal path to recover the numinous for ourselves, shedding our self-limiting beliefs and narcissistic complexes in the process. In tribal cultures, initiation is ultimately a public process that requires an act of witnessing from the collective before it is complete. The visionary knowledge gained through initiatory discipline only becomes meaningful when it is integrated into the community through storytelling, dance, and pageant. In our postmodern world, those who undergo initiation may need to create a shared cultural context to impart the wisdom they have gained from their ordeals. Such knowledge is both a gift and a responsibility: Indeed, if frenzied spirits and sneaky demons are attacking us from beyond the margins of our interpreted world, we may require a revival of shamanic practices to reveal and release them.

THE SEXUAL REVOLUTION, TAKE TWO

For the last few years, I have been exploring the nature of sexuality, love, and relationships, both personally and philosophically. When I separated from my last partner, I realized that I did not feel that monogamy was work- ing for me as a model. Yet I also knew that I craved long- lasting, deep, and sustainable relationships. Since then, I have sought to reconcile my conflicting yearnings, and wondered if other models of relationships are possible or desirable.

Just as we are undergoing a second stage of the process of shamanic initiation that was curtailed at the end of the 1960s, we have entered a wiser and more integrated phase of the Sexual Revolution that crested thirty-five years ago. A more conscious approach to erotic relationships requires a sympathetic awareness of the differences between men and women, and an acceptance of individual distinctions as well. In the 1950s, the scandalous Kinsey Report on human sexuality revealed the vast variety of human sexual experi- ence, and showed that a huge number of people sought intimate contact outside of the confines of their marital relationships. The opening of sexuality in the 1960s led to deflationary decadence in the disco culture of the 1970s, and a pop cultural ambience of constant stimulation and insatiation that the philosopher Herbert Marcuse called "repressive desublimation."

We are still struggling with millennia of negative conditioning—Judeo-Christian guilt, shame, and original sin—around the subject of sexuality. We also belong to a culture that denigrates bodily pleasure and intimacy. In our culture, infants are separated from their parents as soon as they are born and placed in hospital nurseries. In tribal and aboriginal cultures, infants tend to be almost inseparable from their mothers' bodies for the first years of their life. As Robert Lawlor notes in his book *Earth Honoring,* absence of touch in early life may have long-lasting psychological consequences: For aboriginal peoples, happiness is a natural state of being. For denizens of the modern industrialized world, happiness tends to be a distant and almost unattainable goal.

We may not be able to make meaningful progress in the world without a new paradigm for understanding, and embodying, eroticism in its many forms—our dominating attitude toward nature and the Earth is the result of an age-old schism between masculine and feminine energies that requires rebalancing, in the bedroom and the boardroom and the individual psyche. In the twentieth century, psychoanalysts such as Sigmund Freud and Wilhelm Reich realized that misdirection of sexual energy led to buildups of frustration and aggression, both individually and collectively.

Wars and other mass psychoses such as fascism can be linked to sexually repressive or abusive practices in childrearing. The unnatural desire for power over others and control of other people's reproductive functions by fundamentalists and leaders of the radical right could be the result of psychological complexes caused by distortions of sex energy in early childhood, leaving permanent wounds.

Beyond the use of sex for procreation, many spiritual disciplines—including Tantra, Taoism, and Western alchemy—employ sexual energy for spiritual self-creation, channeling the life-force inward and upward through practices involving breath control, vaginal muscular control, semen retention, and visualizations. A disciplined approach to sexual liberation that applies such practices—a ritualized and resacralized realization of Eros—could become an essential aspect of future human development. In an increasingly overpopulated world, a revisioning of sexuality as one pathway to higher consciousness and the Sacred—and of pleasure and happiness as natural aspects of being—could lead to a profound paradigm shift.

For men and women, a transformation of consciousness around sexuality takes different forms. Young men in our culture are conditioned to avoid emotion and intuition and reared on violent video games and horror films that give them a predatory and alienated sense of self, and an aggressive orientation toward sexuality. Young women learn to use their sexual attractiveness as a form of power that can bring them material rewards—and to see their "value" as attached to their desirability. The only way to overcome these deeply ingrained and highly toxic cultural stereotypes is through inner work, warrior determination, and the lived expression of new cultural archetypes.

In a culture that allows for and encourages individual variety in relationship and sexual preferences, some people will remain happily monogamous, but some will prefer to create new models combining personal liberation, self-discipline, and commitment. A deeper integration of masculine and feminine energies could only happen through a compact based on trust, cooperation, acceptance of difference, and a willingness to collaborate in exploration.

Historically, cultural change starts with the few and moves to the many. If a small group—an alternative culture defined by self-awareness and acceptance of difference—makes a real shift in its expression of sexual polarity, love, and relationship dynamics, this new model could quickly become available to a much larger population. Lately, I see many signs of this change happening in the communities that I visit, as if some ancient wall of silence, judgment, and accumulated mistrust between men and women is finally crumbling, allowing for new levels of communion.

LIFE DURING WARTIME

Since my early memories of watching the Watergate hearings on my grandmother's couch when I was a kid, I always felt alienated and disenfranchised from the political process. Although I participated in the occasional protest, even that activity seemed like a meaningless and almost nostalgic gesture to me. My impression of politics was of a rigged spectacle of manufactured consent, a system that allowed only for compromise with or capitulation to the corporate and financial interests that pulled the puppet strings of power. From this perspective, the rise of George Bush seemed natural and inevitable.

After the dissolution—by many accounts, the targeted destruction—of the Radical Left in the early 1970s, many progressives abandoned any hope of transforming the system and turned to other pursuits, from Buddhism to academia to business to literary and creative endeavors. Younger people like myself followed in their footsteps. Despite our uneasy awareness of the destructive effects of U.S. policies across the world, many of us felt that the most meaningful and important work we could do was to change ourselves and actualize our individual potential.

Seeking personal and spiritual fulfillment, we abandoned the sphere of politics to the bureaucrats, PR flacks, and corrupt sycophants who seemed to thrive in it.

In recent years, we have witnessed an accelerating degeneration of the U.S. political system, from rule of law to rule by force. Most of us have avoided confronting the shocking meaning of this change. As Al Gore writes in *The Assault on Reason*, the executive branch, with the complicity of the legislative and judiciary branches, has dismantled much of the separation of powers carefully guaranteed in the U.S. Constitution. At the same time, we have embarked on a "War on Terrorism" that can never be won since our enemy is not a state but potentially anyone who chooses violent means of resistance, along with seemingly unending wars in Iraq and Afghanistan.

We are facing a new situation, and it is critical that we understand the full parameters of what is taking place. The bestselling *Multitude: War and Democracy in the Age of Empire*, by Michael Hardt and Antonio Negri, offers a valuable analysis of current sociopolitical trends. Negri and Hardt are bidding to be the Marx and Engels of our time. Beneath the current crisis of political legitimacy, they see an enormous potential for liberation: the possibility of constituting a global democracy, a planetary "society without a state," with a new set of institutions, legal codes, and social systems.

Hardt and Negri base their analysis on a number of

factors. Following Marx, they believe that changing forms of material production shape human consciousness. In recent times, there has been a shift in emphasis from industrial goods—cars, food, clothing, etc.—to the "immaterial production" of software, media, ideas, images, and affective relationships. Immaterial production tends to be a collaborative and communal process, and one that directly impacts and reshapes our social reality. For instance, a software advance in computer networks or mobile phones gives us new ways to connect with each other, while a popular new film might imprint a new style of interacting. Realizing that conditions have changed since Marx's vision of class struggle and a revolutionary proletariat, Hardt and Negri postulate a global multitude of individuals who communicate through the shared space of the commons and could organize themselves through distributed networks.

Our increasingly networked society points toward a new global orchestration that would eliminate the need for a centralized state apparatus. For this to happen, the multitude would have to realize a shared political project—not just demonstrating against the powers-that-be, as in the massive international protests against the Iraq War, but self-organizing into a truly constitutive body. Although they admit they do not know how this takes place, Negri and Hardt theorize that "insurrectional activity" is no longer divided into successive stages, as in the revolutions of the modern era, but "develops simultaneously." They note,

"Resistance, exodus, the emptying out of the enemy's power and the multitude's construction of a new society are one and the same process."

The sudden fall of the Berlin Wall showed that power structures collapse when the multitude swarms against them. Unfortunately, without advanced planning, such opportunities do not lead to positive outcomes. If we are approaching a similar breakthrough in the West, we require an alternative vision and practical systems that support a shift to a healthier way of life. Some stirrings in this direction include movements like Transition Town in the UK, where local communities are preparing themselves for the effects of peak oil and climate change.

Many of us cut ourselves off from participating in a hypocritical society's power games in order to seek spiritual or creative fulfillment. However, at a time when war has become a "permanent social relation," and the planet's life support systems are in jeopardy, we need to rethink our priorities. Ultimately, our commitment to self-knowledge and our responsibility to society cannot be separated. Reinventing politics through human connections and community actions is a true spiritual path.

THE ALMIGHTY AMERO

These days I feel lost in the immense suffering and madness of our world. Something has snapped in the spirit of the time; events have gone beyond human capacity to control, predict, or even conceptualize. Those who insist they know what is happening are merely pretending, or dissembling. When novelty arises, when old structures disintegrate before new patterns reveal themselves, there are no experts.

Perhaps the best oracles we can consult are systems analysts like Ervin Laszlo. Laszlo studies chaos theory and believes global civilization is a few years away from what he calls "the chaos point." According to Laszlo, we are at a "crucial decision-window" of instability. "When we reach the point of chaos," Laszlo tells us, "the stable 'point' and 'periodic' attractors of our systems will be joined by 'chaotic' or 'strange' attractors." These "strange attractors" will propel us, like booster rockets, to evolutionary development or entropic debauch. In other words, we should prepare ourselves for the unknown and inexplicable.

The current economic crisis provides an intriguing case in point. For those of us with an interest in spirituality and a background in the arts, the conceptual concoctions of modern finance—derivatives, futures, quants, margin calls, and whatnot—can seem as occult as sorcerers' spells. All of these entities are inextricably intertwined in the subprime mortgage market fiasco, which continues to unfold.

Apparently, after stocks dropped in the wake of 9/11, the government stimulated the sluggish U.S. economy by pumping up the housing market. In earlier and more reticent eras, banks and mortgage brokers required collateral before making loans. After 2001, these restrictions were relaxed, bringing the "American Dream" of home ownership—or mortgage debt refinancing—to a wider populace. Loans that began at low interest (only to balloon to high interest later) got handed out to all and sundry. Based on Pollyannaish projections that these high-interest loans disconnected from any tangible assets would be paid back, the subprime mortgages were packaged into "securities" and traded up the financial markets. Several million holders of subprime mortgages are now defaulting on their payments, with more to follow.

Stepping back for a moment, we might see larger historical dynamics at work. Over the last decades, much of U.S. industry was relocated and outsourced to the developing world, leaving a large populace that had little to produce but was still committed to a credit-based, cushy, and consumptive lifestyle. Our financial sector—following the old adage "If you got lemons, make lemonade"—cunningly repackaged the increasing burden of U.S. personal debt,

turning it into a shiny product for the financial markets.
Over the last years, these questionable loans, bundled into
securities, became one of our major exports to the world.
With nothing tangible left to sell, the United States turned
corporate as well as individual debt into its chief export.

It seems inconceivable that the financial institutions
and speculators didn't anticipate large-scale defaults. Perhaps they were counting on the Federal Reserve to bail
them out. During the last months, in fact, the Fed, along
with its European counterpart, has poured hundreds of
billions of newly invented dollars into the financial markets, temporarily stabilizing the system and rewarding the
speculators while doing nothing for the masses of people
facing eviction from their homes and creating the prospect
of hyperinflation.

The Fed, a private institution, "injects liquidity," quips
The New York Times, without needle or syringe. As a Leh-
man Brothers economist notes, "All they do is write down
a number and credit that amount of cash to the bank. It's
a bookkeeping entry." The Fed's miraculous capacity to
create instant cash brings up deeper questions about the
nature of money today—what is it? Delinked from the
gold standard, money is based on little more than our collective belief in it.

In Third World countries, currency crises—often
brought about by predatory speculation—frequently lead
to frozen bank accounts and long breadlines, followed by
a change of currency that creates immense profit for the

banks and the government. Of course, many believe that such a thing could never happen here. Recently, there have been rumors of a plan to form an American version of the European Federation, uniting Mexico, the United States, and Canada under a new currency, the "Amero," and a new constitution, devised by the bankers.

In his essay in the anthology *The Mystery of 2012*, Peter Russell notes that transformations of human culture are built upon each other, with each new revolution requiring exponentially less time to manifest. The Agricultural Age developed over thousands of years, the Industrial Age required a few hundred years, and the Information Age—built upon the manufacturing technologies developed by industrialization—only took twenty years. Russell suggests that the next revolution would be from the Information Age to what he calls "the Wisdom Age." In just a few years, we could shift from a system based on data analysis rewarding corporate and individual greed to one that utilizes human knowledge and foresight to institute a compassionate and equitable planetary culture. The overt irrationality revealed by the current financial crisis might act as a necessary awakening, leading to a large-scale shift in values.

NOVEMBER 2007

"2012" AND THE POET'S DILEMMA

I receive many queries from readers via e-mail, and seek to answer most of them (though not the ones from writers who want my help in finding psychedelics). Sometimes the questions stimulate me to develop my own thinking, such as this recent one from a reader in Portland, on the relation of the ideas in "2012" to contemporary literature. I have put his original e-mail and then my response below.

Question from a reader:

> *Daniel—*
>
> *I recently caught your reading here in Portland, OR, and I have read both of your books twice. Not only have I enjoyed your books, but they have really spoken to me powerfully in a personal way.*
>
> *I am a poet, and I understand your frustration and disappointment with most Western intellectuals. I have always felt that myself, and I feel it now more acutely than ever. I see the value in your critique of Modernism (in* Breaking Open the Head*), and I too feel that poets and artists need to*

move into a new real realm beyond alienation and pessimism.

However, I also have some questions about your position. I read somewhere your criticism of Cormac McCarthy's novel The Road. I just read this novel, and I think it is amazing. I think that you criticized it because you feel that he is imagining a bleak, ruined future, and that he might be in some way contributing to the manifestation of that future by imagining it. Okay, I see your point, just as I see your point in your "fight" with Whitley Streiber.

Here's the problem I have: What is an artist supposed to do? You can only write the visions that come to you. You can't consciously "steer" the material into positive attitudes unless you want your poem or novel to be some sort of propaganda piece, or some sort of fake smile on the face of a suffering man. I do think that an artist is also a person, a spirit, so he or she should be doing inner work to release that pain or hopelessness—to break down the walls that cause alienation. But in the meantime should artists censor their "negative" thoughts?

Also, I have been to Burning Man, and I must say that I was not as impressed as you were. I saw no one there who was anything like the artist that

Cormac McCarthy is. I am open to the possibility that I missed something, that there is something unique to be found there. However, I don't know how you can hold that festival up as some sort of ideal and knock down an artist like McCarthy. Granted, I hope a new Henry Miller better than Henry Miller will emerge. I hope epic poems of joy and celebration can be born out of the shadow of Allen Ginsberg, but I guess I wonder what your thoughts are on this subject. And I wonder if you have reservations about your criticisms of Artaud and Michaux and other brave pioneers. I offer these thoughts with all due respect to the important work you have done and are doing.

My response:

This is a great question, and one that I think about all the time.

I believe that literature and art are crucial in evolving/intensifying consciousness, creating new forms of complex awareness and adding subtle dimensions to human experience. The struggle for women's liberation for instance was voiced in hundreds of years of fiction—Madame Bovary, Anna Karenina, Wuthering Heights, *etc.—which laid the groundwork for a social transformation in the* status of women. Etc. for Dickens and Blake and the awareness of industrialism as a destructive force. I agree that artists can be "the antennae of the race" and the conscience of the species.

However, it is in the nature of art to keep changing, as human consciousness changes. "What is art" is different for each generation—if you reduplicate the style or form of past art, it is not really art in my view but more like craft or self-expression, which is not bad but not transformational in the same way art is.

So we are now responding to radically different conditions than people were before, and the nature and potential for transformative work has also changed. We seem to be in a transition between the bourgeois culture of the last few hundred years—with the novel and lyric poem as its expressive forms—and some other form of social existence that would naturally create different expressive forms.

When I look at the function of contemporary lit and art, mostly it seems to be having a regressive effect, reinforcing the old forms of bourgeois identity with sentimental identifications with the ego. I am very concerned, right now, with the seeming incapacity of most people in our culture to awaken to the dire urgency of our present situation, and to

move from passive contemplation to active engage-
ment. Not just individual works but the entire
construct of the contemporary art and literary
worlds function as another pacifying and dis-
tracting mechanism—someone may read a novel
about war and cry, but that doesn't translate into
organizing to stop the wars we are now waging.
It sometimes seems to me that forces have con-
spired to depoliticize culture and make it socially
irrelevant.

As for The Road, *I agree that McCarthy is a*
terrific writer—I loved Blood Meridian*—who is*
literally "spellbinding" and "entrancing." But what
kind of spell does he cast?

I don't know that I agree with you that you can
"only write the visions that come to you. You can't
consciously 'steer' the material into positive
attitudes . . ." I would just propose to you that this
perspective needs to be questioned and examined.
There may be a kind of romanticizing of inspira-
tion implicit here. This idea might apply to that
romantic/lyrical mode of bourgeois consciousness,
less than to whatever new form of consciousness
and attitude is now emerging.

We can retain the richness and complexity of
the Western psyche and sensibility while integrating
not only the nondual, non-egoic Eastern perspective

but also a sense of creative participation in reality-making that leads to art that illuminates, and helps create a foundation for, the most visionary possibilities of what a human future can be, on the Earth and in the wider cosmos.

At the same time, in this immediate period, I personally would like to see some artists sacrifice their desire for expressing themselves to utilize their gifts for the purpose of planetary (r)evolution. I myself would love to go back to a novel that would take me three to six months to revise, then would come out a year after that, at the earliest. Unfortunately I cannot spare the time, as from my perspective there needs to be an alternative infrastructure in place ASAP, including media and network, that allows for an alternative exchange system, resource sharing, and community organization. Studying works like The End of America *by Naomi Wolf (on parallels between our time and early Nazi Germany),* With Speed and Violence *(on abrupt climate change), and Chris Hedges's* American Fascists, *which looks at the Dominionists' ambition to instate a fascist theocracy in the United States, I think we have no time to waste to work together to create a new social system that supports the evolution and elevation of human consciousness, in the near term.*

It may be that certain types of individual artistic ambitions (which I have as well) could be put on hold until we have transmuted the gathering darkness into light.

Anyway, this is my short answer!

BLACKWATER RUNS DEEP

Naomi Wolf's *The End of America* is a must-read. Powerful and concise, inspiring, and provocative, her book reveals the step-by-step parallels between the extralegal actions of the Bush government and fascist regimes of the past. Apparently, the shift from democracy to totalitarianism follows a predictable, almost predetermined pattern, from the creation of secret prisons and torture chambers, to increasing surveillance of citizens, to the restriction of journalistic freedom and the targeting of key individuals to the subversion of the rule of law.

We have allowed our country to roll far down this slippery slope, and it may require a mass activation of the common will to prevent the next logical—and irrevocable—steps. Reviewing the historical precedents, Wolf notes that the final stages tend to happen suddenly, in the wake of crises that are often artificially engineered by the ruling group. Incidentally, the book goes well with a viewing of *Zeitgeist*, a popular "mythumentary" on the Internet that follows Nietzsche's dictum to "philosophize with a hammer."

Wolf's manifesto sounds a powerful rallying cry. When did our heterogeneous democracy become a "Homeland" (a term previously popularized, Wolf reminds us, by Nazi propagandists in the 1930s)? Why do we find basic constitutional rights such as "peaceable assembly" increasingly demonized by the police in many cities? Why are private mercenary armies, such as the trigger-happy Blackwater, being given free rein, both here and abroad? As individuals and communities and affinity networks, we have to overcome our learned helplessness to rise against the dangerous menace that now confronts us directly.

History informs us that totalitarian regimes inevitably collapse, but not before they inflict vast amounts of destruction. Considering the immediate crisis of climate change and species extinction now facing the biosphere, humanity does not have the time to wait for this cyclical process to fulfill itself, as it has in the past. Somehow we need to jump to the end of the reel—in which the human spirit awakens in victory—without passing through the outdated life-movie montages of secret police raids, demonization of immigrant groups, concentration camps, resource wars, etcetera.

As much as the Bush regime would like to act in a unilateral fashion against Iran, the intricate interweavings of the global economy may prevent our government from launching "World War Four." If the Bush regime were to find a convenient pretext—such as another terrorist attack on U.S. soil—to strike Iran and declare martial law here at home, the United States would become a pariah state, forfeiting its influence on the global stage and inciting domestic economic collapse. It is difficult to see how this could benefit the agenda of anyone—even the most ideologically blinkered NeoCon or bellicose Fox News executive. Potentially, it could lead to a mass defection from the military-industrial sector, precipitating a "fall of the Berlin Wall" scenario in the United States.

For those who would like to advance on the spiritual path, the current crisis in national and global affairs offers a tremendous opportunity for high-speed evolution. It is one thing to contemplate Eastern philosophy from the safety of one's yoga mat, and quite another to realize compassion through acts of self-sacrifice that may lead to direct personal risk, as courageous Burmese monks recently demonstrated. A similar determination was shown by those Western activists who recently unfurled a "Free Tibet" banner at the base camp of the Chinese Olympic team, on Mount Everest.

Lately, I often find myself contemplating the prospect, described by St. Paul, of secret "powers and principalities" acting through our "flesh and blood" leaders and their cronies. There seems to be an occult, hidden dimension to current world affairs that requires not only a rational and strategic response, but also some sort of shamanic channeling of trapped, voracious energies. Efforts such as the Disclosure Project, seeking to compel the release of information about the U.S. government's interaction with "extraterrestrial" or other-dimensional entities, seem less and less far-fetched, as our daily reality melds with sci-fi surrealism.

Beyond the patrolled borders of our increasingly insecure "homeland" is the unified field of our ever more
interconnected "home planet," where there is no "us" versus
"them," no faraway place where we can send our toxic trash
or permit impoverished children to make our clothes for us,
where the sacredness of all life is self-evident. Unfortunately
for the dominant elite, this planetary consciousness seems
an emergent property of our globalized world. Its development cannot be stopped, and it may soon realize itself in
new institutional forms and infrastructures, superseding the
outmoded authoritarian structures that currently control
the movements of capital. From this perspective, "the end
of America," in its current form, may not be a development
to be feared, but an evolution to be welcomed.

ALIEN NATION

While writing my books, I discovered that I was able to keep an open (if skeptical) mind, while exploring subjects that make most people flinch, whether shamanism, psychedelics, or crop circles. These days, I continue to find myself curious about ideas and possibilities that lie even further out on the fringe, partially because of personal experiences I have had, ranging from UFO sightings to inexplicable manifestations. I seem to go through a process in absorbing a new pattern of information, first entertaining it as a vaguely humorous possibility and then slowly acclimatizing myself to it with increasing seriousness.

Lately, two new books have been tantalizing my worldview, suggesting new vistas of possibility. The books are Steven Greer's *Hidden Truth, Forbidden Knowledge* and *Dark Mission: The Secret History of NASA* by Richard Hoagland and Mike Bara. Both books discuss extraterrestrials, alien technology, and secret government coverups, but from different angles. While Hoagland and Bara both offer the perspective that NASA is an occult organization that has concealed its findings of alien artifacts on the moon and elsewhere, Greer makes the case that there are numerous benevolent species of intelligent alien life, at a much higher stage of development than ours, surrounding the Earth and ready to make contact when we are ready. Hoagland and Bara's book is a weird, yet fascinating compendium of geometrical postulates and jarring details. Greer's work, if true, is the best news that humanity has ever received.

Hoagland is well known for his previous work on the Face on Mars, while Greer launched the Disclosure Project, getting military officers and intelligence agents to speak about classified encounters with UFOs and extraterrestrials. These accounts include that of Lieutenant Colonel Robert Salas, who was on duty, sixty feet underground at an ICBM missile base, on March 16, 1967, when a UFO appeared overhead, and the control systems for launching the missiles were suddenly deactivated. "Our missiles started shutting down one by one," Salas reports. "By shutting down, I mean they went into a 'no-go' condition meaning they could not be launched." The same thing occurred at another base, sixty miles away. "So that morning we lost anywhere from 16 to 18 ICBMs at the same time UFOs were in the area and were observed by airmen," continues Salas. Greer proposes that the intelligences behind the UFOs were testing their capacity to neutralize the destructive capabilities of the military, and perhaps also indicating that the military was not going to be permitted to blow the planet to bits.

In *Hidden Truth, Forbidden Knowledge*, Greer tells an

extraordinary personal story of his quest for understanding and his efforts to spread the word. He claims to be able to utilize meditation and psychic protocols to call in UFOs, which can be seen by himself and the people around him. "Any effort to contact ETs peacefully is greatly respected," he writes. He notes that these ships—and the beings that inhabit them—can appear in fully materialized, semi-materialized, or astral form. He describes his meetings with major political figures and his interactions with a shadowy cabal that operates in secrecy and conceals its knowledge of the extraterrestrial presence and its advanced work reverse-engineering alien technology that could solve the world's energy problems, along with many other applications.

I probably speak for many readers when I admit that I still find it hard to imagine that we are on the cusp of a new paradigm of extraterrestrial communion that would literally usher the human race into a new world. Even if I allow myself to imagine it, I still find it a difficult psychological leap. This is the case, even though my own research into the crop circle phenomenon, detailed in *2012*, led me to the hypothesis that the virtuosic formations were not human made, and had to be a communication—a teaching—from other levels of galactic intelligence. The accelerated development of our technology in the last decades suggests that we cannot imagine what a conscious species hundreds of thousands or millions of years more advanced than our own might be capable of creating, or what mechanisms they might use to travel across interstellar distances.

Having noted that, I also admit to being persuaded by the direct simplicity of Greer's book and message, and delighted by his vision of an enlightened future for humanity, where the Earth has become a lightship guiding us on a galactic mission of peaceful exploration. Near the end of *Hidden Truth, Forbidden Knowledge*, Greer offers this meditation: "Sitting quietly now, we see that we are joined by the angelic realm, the celestial beings, the astral worlds filled with our ancestors and with the beings from diverse worlds. And we see that there are extraterrestrial peoples joining us. . . . And we hold within us this thought, and this vision of suffusing the earth in this golden light as it is brought in to this time of peace, and all the wars will be silenced and all the suffering will end." If reality is somehow a cocreation of our consciousness, and we can determine which path to take, then I hope to join Dr. Greer in his reality tunnel.

Recently, while at a Phoenix, Arizona, conference on UFOs, crop circles, alternative archaeology, and other such fringe matters, I encountered, to my surprise, a true American hero. A straightforward and unassuming man whose father was a well-respected Alaskan congressman, Dr. Nick Begich has been waging a long and often lonely campaign to raise the public's awareness of the extraordinary perils and potentials of new technologies that can act upon the brain and influence our cognitive and somatic capacities, often without us knowing about them. At first, many of the military initiatives and scientific research projects described by Dr. Begich sound like science fiction—the stuff of Philip K. Dick's most paranoid visions—but they are quite real, and in many cases already available. A huge trove of documents, articles, and public testimonies assembled by Begich's team can be found at the Web site of the Lay Institute.

Confronted with this information, I was shocked at first, and wondered why it is almost never discussed in the media or public sphere. My next reaction was to want to run away from thinking about it ever again. Unfortunately, as Dr. Begich makes clear, the only protection we have against misuse of these discoveries is an increase in public knowledge and debate about them. The legislative system we inherited from the eighteenth century was not set up to deal with the current scenario, where rapid-fire developments in technology and science have immediate political meaning and potentially great social consequences. It is up to civil society—and us as individuals—to step into this breach. The consequences of not doing so may be severe.

Dr. Begich began his work studying the HAARP (High-frequency Active Auroral Research Program) Project, an array of radio frequency transmitters in Alaska designed to affect the ionosphere, an atmospheric sheath that protects the Earth from solar rays. Beyond potentially influencing missile guidance systems and changing weather patterns, HAARP can also be used, potentially, to affect the brain waves of civilians over a large geographical area, causing inexplicable agitation or aggression by beaming ELF (extremely low frequency) waves or high-frequency pulses beyond the threshold of our auditory capacity. Dr. Begich objects to HAARP because of this capacity, and because it changes the delicate ionosphere. Although we don't know much about the ionosphere, we are treating it as an arena in which to "plug and play" our experimental technologies.

In the last decades, a huge amount has been learned about the electromagnetic environment of the human brain and body. This knowledge, as Dr. Begich discusses in his latest book, *Controlling the Human Mind: The Technologies of Political Control or Tools for Peak Performance*, could lead to tremendous advances in healing and in methods of self-development, or to weapons that "pierce the very integrity of the human being." Potentially, memory, emotion, and cognitive function can be transformed by these technologies.

Dr. Begich isolates a spooky trend in military thought that sees the human being reduced to the status of a "data-processing system" that can be affected or incapacitated depending on the energy inputs it receives. As one article, "The Mind Has No Firewall," from *Parameters*, the U.S. Army War College Journal, put it, "The body is capable not only of being deceived, manipulated, or misinformed but also shut down or destroyed—just as any other data-processing system." Electromagnetic or acoustic energy waves can alter the individual's "hardware system" and manipulate the "data" stored in their psyche. According to Dr. Begich, technologies already exist that can "shift a person's emotions using remote electromagnetic tools," and "transfer sound in a way where only the targeted person" hears a voice in their head.

Interestingly, developments in these areas could lead to breakthroughs in healing, to tools that greatly increase cognitive function and even amplify "abilities of individuals for anomalous phenomena"—psychic capacities—according to a military analyst. Biofeedback techniques have been proven to accelerate skills-based learning and to successfully treat children with ADD. Use of "binaural beats" can harmonize relationships between the two hemi-spheres of the brain, while tools focusing on the energy fields of the body can augment acupuncture and other treatment modalities.

Dr. Begich calls for an end to government secrecy about the study of mind and behavior control techniques. He notes that the area of mind modification technologies is "changing so rapidly that the science is being formed faster than the applications can be fully recognized." Considering the enormous potential of these tools to help liberate the mind or control it at a level beyond anything previously known, the U.S. public should demand to have a rigorous "precautionary principle" put in place.

Philip K. Dick is great fun to read, but few of us would want to live in one of his maniacal, paranoid dystopias. Unfortunately, the powerful knowledge we are now access-ing about the intricate workings of our energetic systems could lead in that direction, if we don't take action.

YOUR MONEY AND YOUR LIFE

Right now, our economic system is teetering as the crash of the subprime mortgage market reveals deeper faults in the banking and insurance industries. Operating with little oversight in the last years, bankers devised complex instruments to make massive loans between financial institutions, generating short-term profits. As liquidity dries up, the banks and insurers are struggling to pay off these debts, forcing the central banks and the Federal Reserve to pump larger and larger sums—hundreds of billions of dollars—into the financial sector.

While this crisis is severe, such paroxysms happen periodically. While some believe this to be a natural process through which the global market corrects itself, others argue that the financial system has underlying design flaws that need to be addressed. Faced with dire consequences of inaction, the financial institutions and government regulators will work together to create a settlement that preserves the illusion of propriety—most likely at great cost to taxpayers and mortgage holders. However they resolve it, this meltdown is an opening for a deeper discussion on how money functions in our society. We have the chance to propose real options that could make the financial system more equitable, as well as sustainable.

We tend to forget that money is, fundamentally, a social agreement, not something natural or elemental. In fact, since the U.S. dollar went off the gold standard in 1971, it is hard to pin down what money actually means, besides virtual bits spinning in the global casinos of the world's financial markets. Bernard Lietaer, a former currency trader and one of the principle architects of the euro, believes that the economic logic inscribed in our currency is the basic cause of unhealthy and predatory aspects of our social system.

In *The Future of Money* and other works, Lietaer analyzes the historical evolution of monetary systems, making a distinction between "Yang" currencies that foster competition and individual wealth and "Yin" currencies that are future-oriented and support the health of communities. Many cultures have used both at the same time, but our currency is purely Yang, inciting cutthroat behavior. It is interesting to consider that "Wall Street" takes its name from the original barrier built by Dutch settlers to keep out Native Americans, whose primary form of exchange was the gift, rather than the market. We have maintained that wall ever since.

Lietaer has proposed a complementary currency, the Terra, that he believes could be used as a global standard for making trades. The value of the Terra is linked to a "basket" of commodities sold on the stock market, and therefore does not float in an abstract void, like today's currencies. Use of the Terra also involves a "demurrage" charge—in essence, negative interest—that increases over time. In other words, the Terra would depreciate in value the longer it was held, and therefore would naturally lead to less hoarding, encouraging capitalists to spread wealth. Ideally, the Terra would be combined with local currency initiatives, such as mutual credit clearinghouses that issue loans without interest and time banks that use an hour as the basic unit of exchange, which keep value circulating within communities.

That the monetary system needs a serious redesign becomes evident when you spend some time pondering the matter. "By controlling the creation and allocation of money, the ruling class maintains near total control over the lives of ordinary people and the resources of the planet," writes David Korten in *The Great Turning*. The basic system by which banks loan money and collect interest on the loans creates artificial scarcity, as the individuals who take the loans have to compete against each other for the extra money, which the banks do not create, to pay back what is owed.

The inherent logic of short-term gain inscribed in our currency system refutes any hope of attaining long-term sustainability. Liberal proponents of globalization, such as the economist Jeffrey Sachs, blinded by a limited model of "progress," fail to see that the form of money we use determines the types of behavior that succeed. What Lietaer offers is an elegant design science approach to this problem. Most likely, such a far-reaching proposal will only be taken seriously as the cracks in our current system become enormous fissures—which should be a matter of time.

The visionary design scientist Buckminster Fuller argued, "All who are really dedicated to the earliest possible attainment of economic and physical success for all humanity" should "shift their efforts from the political arena to participation in the design revolution." These days, we seem to be learning that the design revolution and the political struggle are ultimately the same thing. In a culture that rewards competition, people will fight for their position; in a culture that rewards altruism, people will act with generosity. The realization that human behavior is more or less invariant means that economic and social systems can be redesigned in such a way that collaborative and cooperative behavior is rewarded over selfish action.

OLD STRUGGLES ON A NEW EARTH

Although my book on prophecy and the Mayan Calendar is behind me, I am still approached all the time by people in search of the meaning of the encroaching end date of December 21, 2012. "Is it the end of the world?" reporters ask me on television. In e-mails, I am begged for advice on matters ranging from shamanic ritual to retirement funds, from dealing with extraterrestrials to seeking a safe place to hide out from polar shifts, earthquakes, and superstorms. Meanwhile, academics and self-taught experts send me their pet theories on tribal prophecies, astrological conjunctions, UFOs, Egyptian gods, quantum consciousness, Illuminati conspiracies, free energy technologies, and much more.

My view is that "2012" is useful as a meme if it helps us to catalyze a shift in global culture and consciousness. Rather than fretting about what may or may not happen on that date, we should concentrate on the work that needs to be done now, on an inner as well as outer level. My recent focus has been the outer level, studying social theory and political philosophy. If we were to have an opportunity to transform society, what could that transformation look like in a practical sense? How could it be carried out? I have been reviewing the ideas of thinkers like Machiavelli, Jean-Jacques Rousseau, Thomas Jefferson, Karl Marx, and Hannah Arendt, seeking insight into the nature of politics and power.

How do we bring awareness gained through shamanic practice or yogic discipline back into the gritty realities of political struggle and the fight against global inequity of wealth and resources? It seems there is still a lot of denial among Western mystics and "New Agers," as well as elitism and spiritual materialism. Whether someone does a flawless series of asanas, drinks ayahuasca with twenty different shamans, or visits hidden monasteries in Bhutan has no value as a sign of spiritual attainment. How they live day by day, what they do with the psychic energy and time available to them, and how their work helps to liberate others is what matters.

I see this tendency to ignore the social and political struggle in the works of wildly popular writers such as Eckhart Tolle, who has repackaged Vedanta for the masses. In Tolle's recent book, *A New Earth*, he writes: "We are coming to the end not only of mythologies but also of ideologies and belief systems." According to Tolle, the creation of the "new earth" needs no change in social practices as long as you make "the present moment . . . the focal point of your life." Tolle exhorts his audience to "enjoy what you are doing already, instead of waiting for some change so that you can start enjoying what you do." Whether you are an artist, teacher, Fox News executive, or currency speculator doesn't matter: "The new earth arises as more and more people discover that their main purpose in life is to bring the light of consciousness into this world and so use whatever they do as a vehicle for consciousness." For Tolle, the effort to change our society's inequitable and unsustainable practices has no particular value compared to the paradise of presence.

The popularity of this message is unsurprising. Some political thinkers argue that the adoption of Eastern thought in the West has given people a way to accept capitalism, and "Empire," by finding detachment from it. For the critic Slavoj Zizek, Western Buddhism and Hinduism enable you "to fully participate in the frantic pace of the capitalist game, while sustaining the perception that you are not really in it, that you are well aware how worthless this spectacle really is—what really matters to you is the peace of the inner self to which you know you can always withdraw. . . ." Zizek goes so far as to propose that "the onslaught of New Age 'Asiatic' thought . . . is establishing itself as the hegemonic ideology of global capitalism."

The shift of "2012" could mean that Eastern mysticism, the earth-based shamanism of tribal people, and the West's pursuit of philosophical and scientific knowledge about the world come together to create a new form of consciousness. I suspect the West still has to realize its spiritual destiny—its dharma—in the transformation of matter and the creation of a truly equitable and sustainable world. As the design scientist Buckminster Fuller wrote, "No human chromosomes say make the world work for everybody—only mind can tell you that." We may not need "ideology" anymore, as Tolle says, but we still need good ideas about how we reinvent our society and its institutions to become ethically transparent and sustainable. Rather than escaping from society's problems by embracing pure presence, we can use the awareness gained from spiritual practice to become more effective agents of social change.

The current crisis of the financial markets is rapidly taking on gargantuan proportions. Last weekend saw the emergency sale of Bear Stearns, the fifth-largest financial institution on Wall Street, to JP Morgan for the comparatively paltry sum of $250 million, including its flashy corporate headquarters and thousands of employees. Even this sale only came about because the U.S. Federal Reserve agreed to cover the risks of exposure to creditors, ultimately, in all likelihood, pushing the financial costs onto U.S. taxpayers. An attempted federal bailout of the financial system now seems increasingly unavoidable, as commentators such as Paul Krugman have noted.

At the same time this fire sale was being arranged, I was at the Left Forum at Cooper Union in New York, an annual gathering of Leftist academics and organizers from around the world. The Left Forum featured over one hundred panels on a range of subjects, from water privatization and CIA torture to the leftward shift of South America and many other topics. I had been invited to speak on a panel about indigenous cultures, consciousness, and social transformation—the only place at the Left Forum where social movements were even summarily discussed in relation to indigenous cultures who live "with" the earth, and not "on" it, as my fellow panelist, Tiokasin Ghosthorse, a radio host at WBAI and a Lakota, put it, and non-ordinary states of awareness were given a nod.

During a panel on the "Decline of the Dollar," I was struck by a comment from David Harvey—an éminence grise among Leftist academics and the esteemed author of *The Limits to Capital* and other works—who noted that Wall Street bonuses in January amounted to an astounding $36 billion, despite the heedless actions of the traders and investment houses that caused the implosion of the financial markets. At the same time, due to the subprime mortgage meltdown, more than a million people have already seen their homes foreclosed, with nearly two million more foreclosures coming in the near future, leading to more than three million U.S. citizens' being deprived of their largest and most central asset. What Harvey noted is that, if we ignore the "fetishized mystical language" of the financial elite, "The loss of assets of those three million people is where those $36 billion of bonuses came from."

Apparently, another eight million–plus homes—more than 10 percent of the homes owned in the United States—are now valued at less than the outstanding mortgages owed. What this means is that many of those mortgage-holders may soon find it more sensible to walk away from their property—sending their keys back to the mortgage-issuers as "jingle mail"—than continue to cover their exorbitant debt. As a chain reaction, this will increase the devaluation of U.S. property. At the same time, the next phase of the current economic crisis will extend to other forms of personal debt, such as credit cards. While the U.S. and European Central Banks continue to pour hundreds of billions of dollars into the financial institutions that created this disaster through predatory lending practices, they have done little for the millions of poorer people facing insolvency. As another Leftist economist noted on the same panel, one can only feel "a sense of awe" at the lack of real protest about what is taking place.

Based on my last book, I often find myself looking over my shoulder, wondering if current events fit the prophetic timetable of the Mayan Calendar. Although the validity of Carl Johan Calleman's scholarship has been called into question by John Major Jenkins and others, it is interesting that Calleman predicted the current year (November 2007 to November 2008) to be the year of Tezcatlipoca—sinister deity of black magic and the jaguar—marked by economic collapse, war, and other threats. On the one hand, I have reasons for taking "2012" seriously as a threshold of some type of tremendous transformation, based on my research, my own synchronicities, as well as esoteric and intuitive experiences. On the other hand, studies of the current state of global society insist that massive and accelerating change is unavoidable in all areas of life. The future of humanity is imperiled if we do not transform our social practices and fundamental paradigm within the next years.

My view is reinforced by many recent developments, from the sudden disappearance of honeybees and Chinook salmon to the comment made by a famous financier to a friend, later recounted to me, that currency will have no value in a few years, and the only thing that will be worth anything will be land. One of the depressing aspects of the Left Forum, along with the average age of the audience being well above fifty, was the palpable ambience of failure and defeatism in the crowd. Certainly, the last thirty-five years have been a miserable period for radicals in the United States, who have watched the oligarchy consolidate power, instituting elements of a police state, and holding tight control of the mass media.

Crucial ideas and possibilities can vanish completely for a time—even for an entire generation—before they return with a new force and impetus, to start a new turn on the spiral. This has been the case with shamanic exploration of non-ordinary consciousness, which has made a resurgence in recent years in a wiser and more mature form than in the 1960s. Similarly, it is possible that the moment has arrived when a populist radical movement could reconstitute itself, and this could happen at a rapid pace. Radical movements often burst forth when theorists, sociologists, and academics least expect it. They arise when masses of fed-up people begin to seek direct redress against the system that has exploited and enslaved them.

That our financial system is fixed to reward a minuscule subset of the global population, the "ruling elite" who control the financial sector, is a realization that could begin to permeate the mass consciousness. This awareness can only increase as the destructive delusions of the dominant ideology become more obvious. With the intermeshed networks of contemporary life, a new realization could spread rapidly, along with techniques to confront a system that has failed to protect the poor and the planet. The incredible mismanagement of the earth's precious resources—the squandering of oceans, forests, animals, and air—is an indictment against the current order and its leaders. Although it seems unstoppable, the continuity of this system is a direct threat to future generations.

While most mainstream commentators and even some of the critics at the Left Forum argue that the current implosion of the financial markets is one of the periodic crises of capitalism that eventually gets resolved through institutional measures and bailouts, it actually may be far more than that. This may be neither a crisis of "liquidity" nor even one of insolvency, but a crisis of money itself—in other words, a crisis of faith in the entire belief system of capitalism, which has functioned as a displacement of religion, with money substituting for the banished god. As Karl Marx noted in *The 1844 Manuscripts*, money is "the visible divinity" in a capitalist world:

"By possessing the property of buying everything, by possessing the property of appropriating all objects, money is thus the object of eminent possession. The universality of its property is the omnipotence of its being. It therefore functions as almighty being. Money is the pimp between man's need and the object, between his life and his means of life. But that which mediates my life for me, also mediates the existence of other people for me. For me it is the other person."

When I reread some of Marx last year, for the first time since school, I was startled by the tremendous depth of spiritual insight in his work. The radical essence of his thought has been obscured by the course of history, and by the desire to deny, suppress, and evade it, ever since. Marx saw that the revolutions of the eighteenth century enshrined the rights of the bourgeois individual to compete against others, rather than realizing man as a "species-being" who can only attain freedom through his communion with other men: "None of these so-called rights of man goes beyond the egoistic man, beyond man as a member of civil society, as man separated from life in the community and withdrawn into himself, into his private interest and his private arbitrary will. They see, rather, the life of the species itself, society, as a frame external to individuals, as a limitation of their original independence," he wrote in "The Jewish Question." Freedom was defined negatively, creating a social reality in which each individual had to struggle against others to preserve and increase their private domain.

As David Korten, Bernard Lietaer, and others have written recently, our basic financial system in itself creates artificial scarcity, and induces competition and sociopathic behavior patterns that lead inexorably to disregard of the environment and mistreatment of others. When a bank gives out a loan to someone, it is not creating the extra money that the individual has to make as interest accrues. When it examines that person's credit, it is checking to see if that person has the capacity to compete effectively in the marketplace and come up with the accrued interest, which is imaginary capital at the outset. The individual then competes with others to retrieve the money he owes. Similarly, publicly traded corporations must maximize profits to satisfy shareholders, and this forces an institutional disregard for environmental safeguards and humane practices.

Over the last decade, the deregulation of the financial system "acted like psychotropic drugs on the minds of investors," as one Left Forum panelist noted, unleashing increasingly rapacious and mindless greed. Pushed to its limit, the logic of the system reveals itself in transparent form. The subprime mortgage market offered loans to people with little or nothing in the way of assets or collateral that began at low rates of interest and then ballooned to massive rates later. These predatory loans were then bundled together and sold as securities, given class "AAA" status by regulatory bodies that had little interest in compelling restraint. These securities based on corrupted loans were meshed with other types of assets and securities and sold up the financial pyramid. As in the classic pyramid scheme, when the debtors at the bottom start to default, the rotten edifice comes tumbling down.

At the same time, the crumbling of this scam is revealing deep levels of tulip-style mania in the banks and financial institutions, which had developed highly convoluted mechanisms for extracting profits by lending vast, and nonexistent, sums to each other for short-term periods. While commentators think that the amount of actual wealth that is going to disappear from the world economy is $1.5 to $2 trillion, the amount of imaginary capital traded in rapid fashion to amp up artificial profits was exponentially higher than this number. At a time when credit has evaporated, whoever gets caught holding the IOUs for these massive amounts faces instant insolvency.

It appears that unleashed greed incited by deregulation of the markets has led to a massive implosion of the financial apparatus that may not be fixable within the current system. This crisis may have its roots in the early 1970s, when the United States took the dollar off the gold standard, and the untethered U.S. dollar became the global reserve currency, forcing the developing world to adopt it for international transactions and debt repayment. The building of the World Trade Center towers could be seen as symbolizing the shift of the focus of the U.S. economy from productive industry to finance capitalism, as the parasitical system of speculation on derivatives and currencies became the central wealth-producing engine within the

United States. The lack of U.S. productivity coupled with a virtualized currency with no real-world referent has led to the amassing of extraordinary debt, on an individual and societal level.

The crisis may actually have far deeper roots, going back to the basis of capitalism itself, an economic system that constantly requires new markets to penetrate and cannot sustain itself without continually extending its reach. In a fully globalized world, where there are no new markets to reach or new resources to exploit, capitalism may have reached its natural limit. It is also imprecise to call the current system "capitalist" in a classical sense, as it is actually one where massive subsidies protect vested interests, from agricultural lobbies to oil companies, and the ideal of a "free market" is a convenient fiction.

In a fully globalized world, the Neoliberal model can only perpetuate itself through the types of shock effects described by Naomi Klein in *The Shock Doctrine*, where destruction is encouraged and then seized upon as an opportunity to redevelop and recolonize areas already within empire. One of the panelists at the Left Forum described the mortgage meltdown as a "financial Katrina" that will allow wealthy speculators to take over urban neighborhoods where poor people have suffered mass defaults. The disastrous consequences of rampant privatization are increasingly obvious, as services become weaker, corruption increases, and prices rise.

Considering the extent of delusional capital now

underlying the financial system, it is possible that the current crisis could be pointing toward the end of the current economic paradigm. This could mean a real transvaluation of our world. As Marx points out, the function of money is to transform all qualities to quantities that are ultimately equivalent. Money "is the true agent of separation as well as the true binding agent—the [universal] galvano-chemical power of society," Marx writes in *The 1844 Manuscripts*. Money-as-mediator and ultimate arbiter seeks to reduce all qualities to quantities, and by doing this, reduces everything to sameness, with the Midas touch of nihilism. As Marx notes, love and trust are basic values that elude the mediation of money.

In his great book *The Gift*, Lewis Hyde contrasts our modern market economy with the gift-based economies of tribal and indigenous cultures. He writes, "The desire to consume is a kind of lust. We long to have the world flow through us like air or food. We are thirsty and hungry for something that can only be carried inside bodies. But consumer goods merely bait this lust, they do not satisfy it. The consumer of commodities is invited to a meal without passion, a consumption that leads to neither satiation nor fire." The gift, on the other hand, renews the communal bond, and requires reciprocity as well as trust. Hyde writes:

"The gift moves toward the empty place. As it turns in its circle it turns toward him who has been empty-handed the longest, and if someone appears elsewhere whose need is greater it leaves its old channel and moves toward him. Our generosity may leave us empty, but our emptiness then pulls gently at the whole until the thing in motion returns to replenish us."

If modern society reduces all value to a universal exchange of quantities, indigenous cultures were conscious of qualities that did not allow for perfect equivalences of exchange. Ultimately, it was the state of mind and heart of the giver that mattered, not the objectified value of an object.

The current economic crisis may be resolved—at least temporarily—by an international agreement between oligarchic forces that will lead to some bailouts and a renegotiation, and probable reduction, of American power in the world. Or it may be that the glue that has held together the international monetary order is coming undone, in which case a deeper process of transformation may take place. If this is the case, then the social agreement that is money itself may be up for discussion, and the nature of value may change yet again. In other words, the current economic crisis may represent, not just a reordering of power and finance in the world, but a deeper expression of a crisis of value, and the opportunity to begin the pendulum swing back again, from an economy based on the meaningless exchange of nihilistic quantities to a different model of economy that would require alternative institutions and techniques to support the socially cohesive expression of values-based qualities.

ENLIGHTENMENT REASON OR OCCULT CONSPIRACY?

What holds our world together is not only the laws of physics, but also language, myth, and story. Our narratives create the framework in which our actions and our intentions have meaning, or at least some kind of order. It is very hard for us to live without any coherence at all. It may even be impossible, as our minds immediately begin to weave together some type of fable to support whatever it is we find ourselves doing.

Lately, I find myself switching back and forth between divergent models or myths of reality and seeking to integrate them. One of them is the story of progress and reason, the inheritance of the secular and scientific Enlightenment. The progressive believes that a flawed society can be improved by rational policy and political pressure. The world can be made better for more people, inequities reduced and health care guaranteed. Although he has been strategic in his pronouncements, Barack Obama seems the model of a progressive reformer, promoting the type of sensible policies that led to the New Deal and the Great Society.

The other mythic structure that entices me is occult and conspiratorial. According to this story, there is a hidden agenda beneath the facade of chaotic events. This agenda is orchestrated by "them," that group of elite cabals and secret societies, an amalgam of Free Masons, Vatican priests, the descendants of the Nazi scientists brought to the United States after World War Two, and so on. To approach this concealed dimension of world affairs, to separate accurate insights from disinformation, is extremely difficult, and perhaps impossible. The quest involves long reading lists of small-press and self-published tomes and many hours on YouTube, watching lectures presented by anxious men in drab conferences. From such unreliable sources, one learns that much alien technology has already been recovered and reverse-engineered, that a New World Order of total social control is being orchestrated, that the Ark of the Covenant is a torsion field generator perhaps hidden in the Pentagon, that shape-shifting reptilians are controlling everything, and other tidbits.

Personally, I don't reject the possibility that there is an occult element in global affairs, a distorting factor that makes true understanding difficult to achieve. During my shamanic work, I encountered spiritual and demonic forces, appearing as visions and voices, but also causing effects that seemed to cross the barrier between the psychic and the physical. According to shamanic traditions, spirits operate across the entire field of our world. Rather than a fine-tuned conspiracy of elite cabals, the true story might be far more muddled, with various factions holding pieces of a puzzle, mired in outmoded rituals and incoherent beliefs, lacking shamanic skills. Many of those involved in these cabals may suffer from guilt and fear the consequences if their shadowy actions are revealed to the public.

Out on the esoteric edge of the cultural imagination, one finds an increasing convergence of thought-streams. The works of Steven Greer, David Wilcock, and Richard Hoagland, as well as Nassim Haramein's DVD set *Crossing the Event Horizon* (available at theresonanceproject.org), all suggest that, beyond a certain threshold, technological advances may be linked not just to technical knowledge but to our level of consciousness, requiring higher awareness as well as purified intentions in order to function. As Haramein theorizes, the Ark of the Covenant might have been an actual device preserved from antediluvian civilizations, capable of generating extraordinary amounts of energy—enough to open a passage through the Red Sea—but requiring an initiate on the level of Moses to operate it without causing mayhem. Many of these thinkers offer intriguing scenarios in which alchemical or extraterrestrial possibilities could manifest in tangible forms.

Can someone pursue Enlightenment ideals while simultaneously exploring occult conspiracies? If we avoid becoming obsessive or dismissive, it seems possible to hold contrasting myths or models of reality in our minds at the same time. We can study the Mayan Calendar, extraterrestrials, and Gnostic cosmology while fighting for social and environmental justice, campaigning for political reform, and so on. Whether or not our corrupt system can be changed, we could learn a great deal by joining any valiant effort made in that direction.

For Enlightenment thinkers, the sun symbolized the clear light of reason they adored. The clear light of reason may stream from the sun, but, as the French philosopher Georges Bataille noted, if you turn your gaze upward to look at its source, you find yourself blinded. Those who stare at the sun for too long may go insane. The source of reason in itself produces unreason, blindness, and madness. Reason appears to have an innate contradiction at its center. Reason, by itself, may not be enough to get us out of our planetary plight. If spiritual forces operate within our world, then meaningful social change requires, along with political reform, initiatory processes and shamanic practices that could, perhaps, open our minds to new myths of reality.

THE FUTURE OF PSYCHEDELICS

The 2008 World Psychedelic Forum was an almost shockingly respectable affair. Held in Basel, Switzerland, in a spacious convention center next to the five-star Swissôtel Basel, the event drew 1,500 visitors for a two-day symposium on the past and present state of psychedelic thought and research. Despite flashes of eccentricity and Day-Glo, you could have easily thought you were at a conference for alternative medicine or some abstruse but uncontroversial hobby. I felt honored to be one of the speakers, part of a high-profile group that included the Czech LSD researcher and theorist Stanislav Grof; Ralph Metzner, a well-known author and teacher and one of Leary's original partners at Harvard; botanists Dennis McKenna, Christian Raetsch, and Kat Harrison; MAPS director Rick Doblin; anthropologist and author Jeremy Narby; visionary artists Alex and Allyson Grey; and many more.

The Gaia Media Foundation organized the forum, following on its successful LSD conference, marking the hundredth birthday of LSD chemist Albert Hofmann, two years ago. The 2008 event mingled nostalgia and insularity, futurism and hope, in equal measures. On the nostalgia side, Timothy Leary's archivist Michael Horowitz mounted an exhibit of psychedelic art and media imagery, much of it from the heyday of late-sixties flower power, while Carolyn (Mountain Girl) Garcia gave a heartfelt speech about her journeys with the Merry Pranksters and the early Haight-Ashbury days of the Grateful Dead. Although Hofmann is still alive, he declined to attend the festivities. A proper Swiss bourgeois, he didn't approve of the conference being scheduled for Easter weekend.

Sixty-five years since Hofmann's first accidental dose, new frontiers in psychedelic research are opening up, represented at the Forum by an array of therapists and scientists from institutions across Europe, the United States, and Canada. The medical establishment imposed a thirty-five-year blockade on psychedelic research with human subjects; today, these experiments are permitted once again. In Switzerland, a new study explores LSD as a tool of psychotherapy—the first such study to be allowed since the early 1970s. After years of persistent effort, the Multidisciplinary Association of Psychedelic Studies (maps.org) has succeeded in shepherding a number of projects through the regulatory system. Studies under way in the United States include research on use of psilocybin as a treatment for cluster headaches, and on MDMA (Ecstasy) as a treatment for post-traumatic stress disorder, a complex that is haunting tens of thousands of veterans as they return from the Iraq War.

Today, it is possible that psychedelics can be reintroduced into mainstream culture, not as drastic catalysts of social upheaval but as tools that help people overcome serious problems. In the future, MAPS sees itself becoming a "nonprofit pharmaceutical company" that distributes psychedelics to qualified professionals. On a deeper, almost subconscious level, cultural and political resistance to the scrupulous study and use of psychedelics seems to have dissipated. A recent study conducted at Johns Hopkins, giving psilocybin to subjects who had never taken a psychedelic before, found that most subjects had long-lasting positive changes in their worldview. CNN and *The Wall Street Journal* gave prominent coverage to the results of this study.

Beyond the scientific framework, there is compelling anecdotal data on the benefits of psychedelic use for creative processes, intellectual work, and personal development. Recently, British newspapers reported that Francis Crick may have been taking low doses of LSD around the time or a few years after he discovered the double helix shape of the DNA molecule (although he refused to allow this to be published before his death). The Nobel Prize–winning biochemist Kary Mullis openly discussed the inspiration he gained from psychedelics. Many pioneers of the Internet and the personal computer experimented with mushrooms and LSD. And of course, the psychedelic-inspired music, film, literature, and visual culture of the late 1960s remains anthemic, as well as iconic.

During his speech at the conference, Dr. Tom Roberts, a psychology professor at Northern Illinois University, proposed that the rediscovery of psychedelics in modern culture is creating a "second Reformation." During the first Reformation, the Bible, which was only available to a priest class able to read Latin, was translated, printed, and distributed to the masses, who were then able to read and interpret the "word of God" for themselves. By providing direct access to the mystical experience described in sacred texts from around the world, this "second Reformation" will, eventually, eliminate the need for a priest class that stands between the individual and personal revelation. In the past, humans needed a long time to make such a deep shift in paradigm—the first Reformation developed over a few hundred years. Today, the instantaneous sharing of new ideas and information through the Internet could support a far more rapid change in perspective.

At this point in time, those of us who see validity in the psychedelic experience can feel cautiously optimistic that we are reaching a tipping point in cultural perception. The discourse around hallucinogens has become far more sophisticated and measured than it was a generation ago. While Timothy Leary argued that psychedelics were a short-cut to "enlightenment" and that everyone should "turn on" and "drop out," researchers today consider psychedelics to be powerful tools that have negative effects if used improperly, like all tools. But these substances may also have tremendous benefits for the individual and society, when we become mature enough to make proper use of them.

NONVIOLENT ACTION AS
SPIRITUAL PRACTICE

This spring, New York City hosted a series of events to commemorate Mahatma Gandhi's movement of satyagraha, "truth-force," the use of nonviolent activism as a political technique. Gandhi has become one of those saints from the distant past whose name is frequently invoked without thought to the nature of his achievements. When we consider the violence saturating the world today, it is remarkable to recall that satyagraha triumphed over the British Empire, winning independence for India. This victory required great sacrifice and acceptance of privations, violent attacks, and imprisonment on the part of many thousands, Hindus and Muslims alike, who joined his movement.

Gandhi's spiritual practice of active nonviolence is very different from the passive doctrine of ahimsa, "nonharming," that has gained popularity in the yoga community of the West. Ahimsa is ideally suited for a situation where nobody is seeking to cause you harm. If you find yourself in imminent danger, or caught in a larger system of oppression, different measures need to be taken. Techniques of satyagraha can include protests, strikes, work stoppages, slowdowns, civil disobedience, and so on. "No government can exist for a single moment without the cooperation of the people, willing or forced, and if people withdraw their cooperation in every detail, the government will come to a standstill," Gandhi noted.

Gandhi believed spiritual concepts had no value unless they were directly applied to our situation on the earth. "Without a direct active expression of it, nonviolence, to my mind, is meaningless," he stated. The New Age movement in the West has allowed for a convenient schism between personal practices and principles. Among the privileged elite, many people who profess spiritual beliefs succeed within a system that violates their ideals. Among people I know, it still seems "cool" to be a yogini and vegan while modeling for cosmetics companies with shoddy environmental records, or to practice Buddhist meditation while writing ad campaigns for corporations that use Third World sweatshop labor.

At St. John's Cathedral near Columbia University, an evening was dedicated to satyagraha and climate change, featuring music by Philip Glass and Odetta. The suggestion of this event was that the nonviolent methods developed by Gandhi could be used to oppose governments and corporations that have failed to address this great threat to humanity. Such a movement does not seem to be arising at this present time, and instituting it presents unique challenges.

While racism or imperialism are obvious enemies, many of the issues facing us now are more intangible. As Buckminster Fuller wrote, "No human chromosomes say 'make the world work for everybody'—only mind can tell you that." It would be reasonable for people to demand a far more equitable distribution of wealth and resources, reduction of labor time, immediate world peace, public oversight of science and technology, and a rapid transition to sustainable practices and alternative energy sources. A global "Marshall Plan" to reduce carbon emissions and stabilize the climate system is needed, along with a deployment of techniques to reverse pollution of the biosphere. The universal nature of such demands makes them seem unrealizable, although their logic is not hard to grasp.

When we consider the digital networks that spread information and ideas across the planet instantly, the chance for a global satyagraha movement to arise cannot be dismissed. The vast protests against the Iraq War in 2003 appeared suddenly, and disappeared just as quickly. Another inciting event, such as a war or tactical strike, might incite a wave of popular resistance that would not end after a march or two, but swell into a real movement of civil disobedience.

Nonviolence can only succeed when peace is converted from a passive wish to a constant activity. As Mark Kurlansky writes in *Non-Violence: The History of a Dangerous Idea*, a well-organized nonviolent movement poses a greater threat to an oppressive power than any other form of resistance. As appears to have happened recently in Tibet, oppressive regimes will seek to provoke nonviolent resistors into violating their creed, so they can take drastic reprisals. "History teaches over and over again that a conflict between a violent and a nonviolent force is a moral argument," Kurlansky writes. "The lesson is that if the nonviolent side can be led to violence, they have lost the argument and they are destroyed."

We now know that the earth's climate system does not change slowly, but goes through radical and sudden breaks. Glaciologists found that "roughly half of the entire warming between the ice ages and the postglacial world took place in only a decade," writes Fred Pearce in *With Speed and Violence: Why Scientists Fear Tipping Points in Climate Change*, with a temperature increase of 9 degrees during that time. In the past two centuries, humanity has increased levels of carbon in the atmosphere by about a third. Our continued tinkering runs the risk "of producing a runaway change—the climactic equivalent of a squawk on a sound system."

In the United States alone, tens of millions of people now practice spiritual disciplines such as Buddhism and yoga, shamanism and Qi Gong. If this conscious and privileged subset were to band together, we could apply our spiritual ideals in a social movement. We could use the techniques of active nonviolence practiced by Gandhi and Martin Luther King, Jr., to confront our out-of-control military complex and corporate structure, and demand the changes necessary for the safety of our children and our own future survival.

2008: THE RETURN OF CHICKEN LITTLE

A few years ago, while working with shamans in the Amazon jungle of Brazil, I channeled a prophetic voice that announced itself as Quetzalcoatl, the Mesoamerican deity. The voice insisted a great karmic reckoning was on its way. These days, I often feel more like Chicken Little, seeking to warn people that the sky above them is starting to fall. The more I explore what the near future may bring, the more I feel like running for cover.

Dmitry Orlov's *Reinventing Collapse* argues that the United States is headed for an imminent economic meltdown that will be as devastating as the fall of the USSR in the 1990s: "Try to form a picture in your mind: it is a superpower, it is huge, it is powerful, and it is going to come crashing down," he writes. "You or me trying to do something about it would have the same effect as you or me wriggling our toes at a tsunami." According to Orlov, an engineer and peak oil theorist, the causes of this crash include ideological gridlock, the entrenched corruption of our corporate state, the massive debt piled on by heedless U.S. policies, and our utter dependence on a rapidly diminishing supply of fossil fuels.

Predicting mass bankruptcy, hyperinflation, and resource shortages, Orlov recommends stockpiling items that can be bartered on the black market, such as razors, condoms, and liquor; strengthening local communities; and learning how to grow your own food. "For most people in the U.S., rich or poor, life without money is unthinkable," he notes. "They may want to give this problem some thought, ahead of time."

The most penetrating inquiries into our immediate future seem to be coming from small press writers such as Orlov. His book is published by New Society Press, which specializes in studies of our unfolding debacle and pragmatic tactics for dealing with its unavoidable fallout. Another meta-perspective is provided by Alexis Zeigler's *Culture Change: Civil Liberty, Peak Oil, and the End of Empire*. Zeigler's bracing little screed explores the connection between biofuel production and world hunger and argues that ecological crisis will lead to increased authoritarianism in the short term.

While Zeigler describes the dangers ahead, he is more optimistic than Orlov in that he sees the possibility of a mass activation of social awareness and a shift to more sustainable patterns. "The solution to changing the Western lifestyle is the simple impossible act of creating social networks that build social support outside of the mainstream in the context of a truly sustainable society," he writes. Both writers foresee the necessity of adapting communal lifestyles to stretch increasingly scarce resources.

Interestingly, Orlov proposes that the friendly American mentality is much better suited for communal life than the surlier Russian psychology.

I tend to agree with these authors that the next few years are going to see extraordinary and even unprecedented hardships as many negative factors combine in unexpected ways to amplify each other. In the United States, as the going gets rough, there is certainly the potential for a further degeneration into a hyper-controlled security state. The horrific development of "disaster capitalism" based on Milton Friedman's economic doctrine is well-documented in Naomi Klein's *The Shock Doctrine*. The last decades have seen a massive transfer of assets from the poor and middle class to the wealthy elite, who are now contracting with private security firms to guard and rescue them in the event of social or ecological catastrophe.

At the same time, there are many positive developments that could counteract the doom-and-gloom. The increasing ease with which groups of people, ranging from small communities to massive crowds, can self-organize and mobilize through the Internet, using new Web 2.0 tools, is viewed as a revolutionary development in Clay Shirky's *Here Comes Everybody*. My hypothesis, shared by many, is that there is also a change happening in human consciousness, with increasing numbers of people recognizing psychic capabilities and undergoing initiations that lead to mystical insights, compassionate openings, and awareness of deeper levels of unity. It is interesting that our new media technologies amplify our awareness of interconnectivity, a once rarefied spiritual insight that is now becoming apparent to many people.

The material crisis we face is an expression of a spiritual crisis that requires a deep transformation of values and habits. As our current civilization melts down around us, my personal hope is that those people who have initiated themselves through spiritual practices—whether yoga, meditation, shamanism, martial arts, or other disciplines—will step forward as leaders, helping the multitudes who have not been prepared for such a shift. A prudent course of action in the near term might involve a process of self-education and study in sustainable techniques, securing access to clean water and locally grown food, exploring "off the grid" tools and alternative energy sources, while deepening one's spiritual practice in preparation for greater changes ahead.

As Charles Darwin wrote, "It is not the strongest of the species that survive, nor the most intelligent, but the most adaptive to change." As the pace of change increases rapidly, we have a great opportunity to practice non-attachment, to pare down to essentials, and to learn by doing. Rather than ignoring our intuition and remaining complacent, it would be best to face the future and make substantive changes in our lifestyles and expectations right now, while encouraging our friends and communities to do the same.

As I write this, many progressives have lost hope that a
Barack Obama victory will mean a real change in direction
for this country. Obama now supports the death penalty
as well as retroactive immunity for telecommunication
companies that gave data on U.S. citizens to government
intelligence agencies, violating our constitutional rights.
Worst of all, Obama offers no far-reaching plan of action
to address the dire ecological crisis—resource depletion,
species extinction, climate change—that threatens our immediate future. At a time when we need leaders who speak
truth to power, he is playing the old political game.

What kind of policies would offer a meaningful response to our current situation? Unfortunately, the changes
we need seem so far beyond the limits of current political
discourse that it might be laughable if it weren't tragic.
With the earth's population expanding and burgeoning
middle classes in China and India demanding a fairer
share of dwindling resources, the American lifestyle needs
to be radically downscaled. We are 4 percent of the earth's
population consuming 25 percent of its energy, and this
cannot continue.

Currently, the U.S. government borrows $2 billion a day to stay afloat, and spends an estimated $1 trillion a year on our military. This extraordinary sum should be used to transition to alternative energy technologies, develop sustainable eco-villages and eco-cities, and deploy natural techniques of bioremediation. With peak oil looming, we need a national program to promote communal living and sharing of resources, along with a movement toward relocalization and decentralization of food, goods, and energy production. We should reduce our dependence on the automobile and rebuild railways, trams, and other forms of mass transportation.

Around the globe, it has become clear that "free market capitalism" (a protectionist racket, for the most part) benefits a tiny elite and works against the interests of the vast majority. A mix of capitalist incentives and socialized policies, as in Northern European countries, can create a cohesive society that protects the local environment. The U.S. model of endless economic growth based on absurd indicators such as the Gross Domestic Product must be rejected. New measurements can promote a higher quality of life rather than a greater quantity of economic transactions.

The effort to secure oil reserves in the Middle East through military dominance is doomed to failure. We are in danger of seeing our overstretched military begin to crumble, much like the far-flung Roman Empire collapsed due to depleted resources and rampant corruption. The best option would be an immediate shift to a strategy of demilitarization and pacification. The United States could regain its stature by leading the world in the dissemination of nonviolent techniques. Our military bases could become training centers for meditation, permaculture, and other skills useful to local communities across the earth. It seems obvious that establishing a global culture of peace is the only path toward enduring security.

Civil society must be empowered to oversee the development of all research in science and technology, taking a long view that encompasses future generations. The legal form of the corporation must be changed so that profits no longer take precedence over people or places. We should pay elected officials a modest, working-class wage and make them directly accountable to their constituents, who could fire them as soon as they renege on campaign promises.

Creating a sustainable society requires a far more equitable distribution of wealth. Tax structures should be changed to reflect this. We may also require a deeper change in the structure of the monetary system, including a return to local currencies. The "War on Drugs" needs to end, with personal drug use decriminalized. The prison population can be offered employment in agriculture, as the shift to small-scale organic farming will require a large workforce, following Cuba's model.

Facing the severity of our ecological crisis requires a rapid development of collective intelligence and social awareness in the U.S. population. The Internet could provide a collaborative infrastructure to support rapid transition. The mass media could disseminate an understanding of critical issues around sustainability, and retrain people's behavior patterns. For this to happen, the corporate stranglehold on news and information needs to be broken. This will require a revival of public broadcasting and, perhaps, a partial nationalization of the broadcast spectrum.

The American diet must also change radically. Rigid limits must be put on personal consumption of meat, which requires massive inputs of water and grain, as well as fish, since the oceans are almost empty and aquaculture creates toxic waste. The materialism of America can be superseded by a new focus on creative expression and spiritual development, returning us to the "can do" spirit of earlier epochs of American life and reviving the Transcendental ethos of Emerson and Thoreau.

All of this may sound impossibly idealistic. However, it is far more idealistic to believe that we can continue on our current path without massive social and economic breakdowns and increasingly severe ecological disasters. What we have been conditioned to want as individuals becomes immaterial when the planet is no longer willing to support our way of life.

ABSORBING ORBS

This summer, I visited Glastonbury, the New Age epicenter of England, to speak at a "Great Mysteries" conference about orbs. Orbs are best known as those mysterious balls of light that started to appear on digital photographs fifteen years ago, though some claim they can see them with the naked eye as well. Orbs have spawned an enthusiastic subculture of people who believe the blobby wisps are not dust particles or lens anomalies, but angels, spirits, other-dimensional beings, and so on. Although I am now an accredited orbs expert, I remain agnostic on the subject. In this area, one encounters the same difficulties in establishing a methodology as one does with other phenomena that float on the outer edge of cultural possibility, such as UFOs, crop circles, occult conspiracies, miraculous appearances of the Virgin, and so on.

The Orbs Conference offered an eccentric collection of testimonies, channeling, scientific research, and slide shows. My favorite take on the orbs came from William Bloom, a local mystic, who claims he has telepathic chats with the spheres. The orbs told him they work like "a cloud or a flock," and visit us to "support group consciousness."

According to the orbs, "As we touch your individual psyches you begin consciously to experience yourselves as intimately connected with all other life-forms on this planet and throughout the cosmos." A physicist who connected two cameras to take simultaneous photographs found that orbs would only appear on one or the other camera. While he took this as evidence of their quantum subtlety, it could suggest spoof rather than proof.

In my talk on the orbs, I downplayed the question of the orbs' authenticity to take a sociological approach. A postmodern phenomenon, the orbs only appeared in our world due to new technology, digital media, and social networks like Flickr, or blogs where people share orb images. As our evolving social technologies keep bringing us together in unexpected ways, Bloom's transmission about "group consciousness" is thought-provoking. As media theorist Clay Shirky explores in *Here Comes Everybody*, new social tools are making it possible for previously unconnected groups of people to suddenly behave like a "cloud or a flock," when their interests coincide.

The orbs express a cute, trickster element by redirecting our attention. Most people first discover orbs when they are trying to photograph something else—friends at a party, a politician, their cat. Once captivated by the odd spheres floating through their images, their perspective changes: What seemed most important becomes marginal, and vice versa. A friend of mine once suggested that the year 2012—end date of the Mayan Long Count—might be when the center and the periphery of our attention switch places. The areas that our culture now finds important—such as possessions and wealth—might become marginal, while other areas, such as the development of soul and the ability to perceive subtle energies, will take on greater significance.

Although I do not pretend to have certainty in this area, I find the theories of Dr. Alexey Dmitriev, a Russian scientist, to be highly intriguing. Dr. Dmitriev believes that our entire solar system is undergoing a phase transition, entering a region of the galaxy saturated with more intense cosmic energies. He has documented changes on other planets and moons around our solar system, some of which are developing atmospheres or experiencing polar reversals. One way this phase transition is manifesting on earth is in increasing "vacuum domains" such as tornadoes, which are occurring with greater frequency. The orbs might be linked to this transition to a higher-energy state, as plasma-based vacuum domains that appear for an instant before spinning away. Plasma is the most unstable form of matter, and could be responsive to psychic energy—the orbs seem drawn, if not produced, by conscious intent. In photographs, they appear with greater frequency and in greater numbers at celebrations, group meditations, weddings, and so on.

It can seem a bit reductive to seek to explain phenomena— such as the gregarious orbs—that reside at the periphery of our awareness. What is an explanation, in any case?

Generally, it is a like cheap magician's trick that pretends to make the Mystery disappear by covering it with language. As a phenomenon, the mass interest in the orbs suggests we are going through another wave of "Spiritualism," a movement that swept the United States and Europe in the 1890s, bringing with it a wave of aura photography, levitating mediums, and other anomalous events. Only the future will reveal whether the orbs reflect a deeper development of psychic awareness, or whether they are a fad that will soon trail off into the ether, from whence they perhaps came.

TRANSITION TOWN

Toward the end of his life, Thomas Jefferson realized that the American Revolution had failed to provide institutional mechanisms to keep the creative spirit of insurrection alive in the populace. He wanted to institute a township system, giving more self-determination to local communities, or "elementary republics." For Jefferson, the goal of a democratic republic was to make everybody feel "that he is a participator in the government of affairs not merely at an election one day a year but every day; where there shall not be a man in the state who will not be a member of some one of its councils great or small, he will let the heart be torn out of his body sooner than his power wrested from him by a Caesar or a Bonaparte." He worried that the representational government devised by the federalists had deprived people of a public space where their freedom could be meaningfully exercised.

Unlikely as it seems, the Jeffersonian model may get its chance in the next few years, due to the converging forces of peak oil and climate change. Richard Heinberg, author of *Powerdown: Options and Actions for a Post-Carbon World*, calls the project that confronts us "a species-wide effort toward self-limitation." Such a project requires global co-ordination and cooperation to reduce resource consumption and energy use, while industrialized countries "forgo further conventional economic growth in favor of a costly transition to alternative energy sources." For Heinberg's "powerdown" approach to work, the United States would quickly decentralize food, energy, and industrial production, and return a great amount of decision-making power to local communities.

While admitting that these proposals seem unlikely in the current geopolitical climate, Heinberg believes they are not impossible: "In order to save ourselves, we do not need to evolve new organs; we just need to change our culture. And language-based culture can change very swiftly, as the industrial revolution has shown." In *Culture Change: Civil Liberty, Peak Oil, and the End of Empire*, Alexis Zeigler similarly argued, "The solution to changing the Western lifestyle is the simple impossible act of creating social networks that build social support outside of the mainstream in the context of a truly sustainable society."

We are facing a difficult transition that needs to occur at a rapid pace if we don't want to experience dire consequences. According to Robert Hirsch, author of a 2005 Department of Energy report on peak oil, the problem is "much worse than the worst that we could think of. . . . The risks to our economies and our civilization are enormous, and people don't want to hear that." We use oil to make our food and most of our consumer goods. David

Korten notes, "Without oil, much of the capital infrastructure underlying modern life becomes an unusable asset, including the infrastructure of suburbia, the global trading system and the industrial food production, processing and distribution system."

The downsizing of American life is going to be a hard sell, but not necessarily an impossible one. Depending on how it is presented to us, we might see reconnecting to land and community as an improvement over our current alienated state. As Rob Hopkins writes in *The Transition Handbook: From Oil Dependency to Local Resilience*, "It is one thing to campaign against climate change and quite another to paint a compelling and engaging vision of a post-carbon world in such a way as to enthuse others to embark on a journey towards it." Hopkins proposes that cities might be transmuted from "large, bland places with a few 'entertainment' venues, to diverse places with gardens, ponds, artworks, more opportunities for meeting and working with people and generally more to see and do," where people had "less reason to travel to be entertained."

The English "Transition Town" movement prepares local communities for the changes that are coming. It is a highly successful and well-developed grassroots initiative ongoing in over sixty towns and small cities across the UK. Transition Town groups share information, meet with local government officials, and organize courses in basic skills—from boot making to identifying local medicinal herbs—that will be needed again as fuel supplies diminish. They have also experimented with issuing local currencies that help to keep wealth within a community.

It may seem a daunting and unenviable challenge to convince people to adopt such a program—one that includes personal and community sacrifice, a downshift into reduced patterns of consumption, and the surrendering of some forms of autonomy for the general good. On the other hand, previous generations of people just like you and me have mobilized for wars and performed enormous acts of service and self-sacrifice.

Hopkins, one of the creators of the program, writes, "Rebuilding local agriculture and food production, localizing energy production, rethinking health care, rediscovering local building materials in the context of zero energy building, rethinking how we manage waste, all build resilience and offer the potential of an extraordinary renaissance—economic, cultural and spiritual." Almost any community can make use of the Transition Town model, which offers a holistic approach and practical tools for raising social awareness about the crises we face. Ironically, the virtual Internet provides the perfect mechanism for distributing tools and practices for rebuilding local communities around the world, instantly, so they are available as soon as anyone feels inspired to make use of them. Thomas Jefferson would be proud.

PUT A FORK IN IT (THE GLOBAL FINANCIAL SYSTEM IS DONE)

I have developed the late-night habit of obsessively tracking through articles and reports on the global financial system. It appears that the patient is in the throes of a massive heart attack, after years of abuse and hyperactivity, and all attempts at resuscitation are failing quickly. Recent highlights include:

1. A LEAP 2020 report argues that the United States could be forced to default on its debt, and the *Telegraph* agrees that the current infusion of hundreds of billions of dollars from European and American central banks will only delay the next level of collapse, potentially leading to martial law in the United States and many European countries within a short timeframe.

2. An editorial from Sunday's *New York Times* anticipates an upcoming "rash of corporate bankruptcies" that will be "very bad news" for stockholders, employees, and lenders.

3. An analysis concludes that the $700 trillion

derivatives market is about to melt down, along with thousands of hedge funds, according to *The Guardian*.

4. Meanwhile, the lack of credit is crippling export of basic goods from the "developing world," endangering the lives of millions of people whose existence depends on our purchase of their products. A mega-crisis caused by the greed of the rich is destroying the lives of the poor.

All of this data, and much more, strongly suggest that the global financial system, in its current form, cannot be salvaged. At best, we may have a few years before the system fails us. We tend to forget that money is a social agreement, not a natural thing. If basic trust in our institutions evaporates, money, in its current form, will become worthless.

Since previous human societies used different mediums of exchange—such as the gift economies of tribal people— it is quite possible that our current form of money could be replaced by a different set of mechanisms for exchanging value. Few people in our society have pondered this prospect. Nobody has developed a working contingency plan that addresses all of the problems we face in a systemic way. In order to do this, we need a "comprehensivist" approach— think Buckminster Fuller meets Machiavelli—that takes into account all of the essential elements, including human psychology and design science. We need a new model, along with a message that appeals to the vast majority of global stakeholders, one that speaks to both the wisdom and madness of crowds.

If the global financial system goes down, what will have value, and how will value be exchanged? How will we maintain the inextricably complex support systems that sustain billions of human lives in our globalized world? How can we evolve to a new ecological and ethical paradigm instead of degenerating into warring factions? We'd better come up with answers to these questions, as quickly as possible. It may help to study recent case studies, such as Cuba and Argentina, which demonstrate how complex modern cultures can reorganize manpower and resources when they have been cut off by the global system.

We can only find the answers when we share a coherent understanding of how we arrived at this juncture. With a crisis as massive and multidimensional as this one, it seems difficult to find the proper framework to interpret and understand it. While one immediate cause was the overvaluing of housing and the packaging of subprime mortgages into complex financial instruments, that was ultimately only a symptom of deeper structural flaws. For the last decades, financial speculation was used to extract value and tangible assets from the poor and middle class, and transfer them to the wealthy. This greed-based system is self-destructing in agonizing slow motion, as happened previously when the "Roaring Twenties" led to the Great Depression and New Deal.

The modern West created an economic system fundamentally based on the creation of debt. Capitalism requires constant expansion and exploitation of new markets in order to maintain itself. Economists have ignored the hard limits on planetary resources when calculating future potential for development. It was an absurd, almost cartoonish error to believe that we could continue limitless growth on a finite planet.

Capitalism has tremendous dynamism but is inherently unstable. In the future, we will look back to realize that capitalism was a transitional system, unifying the world into a single market and communications grid, before being replaced by a more durable and sustainable economic order. Ironically, considering his repudiation in recent decades, much of Marx's analysis is proving accurate and prescient.

On another level, we can see that the current global crisis has been forced by the mind-set of domination and competition that reflects our immaturity as a species. The Darwinian notion of the "Survival of the Fittest" was an imposition of our competitive and egocentric worldview onto the natural world. As most biologists now see it, healthy ecosystems are based on complex patterns of cooperation and interdependence. As the WBAI talk-show host Tiokasin Ghosthorse notes, humanity must shift from living "on" the earth, to living with the earth. We are not outside of nature, but a part of it.

Put in the simplest terms, then, our global society is going to have to undergo a quite sudden transition from competitive and possessive behavior to cooperation and sharing if we want our species to survive, let alone thrive, into the future. Considering the ecological crisis of species extinction and climate change and the fragility of our support systems, this change has to happen in an extraordinarily compressed timeframe. What we don't have yet is a realistic plan of action that gets us from here to there.

BREAKDOWN AND BREAKTHROUGH

Witnessing the unraveling of the global financial system, I find myself gripped by contrasting emotions. While part of me feels like heading for the hills and hoarding cans of sardines, another part of me is giddy, almost celebratory. The tyrannical rule of Wall Street is ending, along with the self-serving free market ideology of Neoconservatives. The massive amounts of fictitious capital created by our corrupt financial system must be destroyed, so we can address our immediate situation on this planet.

I feel sorry for the millions of people who may suffer during a transition that could be extremely difficult. On the other hand, our rapacious economic system is tearing apart the integrity of the biosphere, threatening our future as a species. Taking a wider perspective, we can see that a new social structure that creates sustainable patterns of behavior is necessary, if we want our descendents to continue on the earth.

In my last book, I looked at many predictions of systemic financial dissolution at this time. I discussed the possibility that a financial H-bomb could melt down the economic system while leaving the "tangible assets"—people, infrastructure, land—still standing. I suggested that this could be the best thing to happen to our world. Such a systemic collapse is a tremendous opportunity to change the direction of our society. Those who believe that civilization can be run according to different principles—humane, equitable, and collaborative ones—need to step forward now with concrete proposals, and put ideals into practice.

Several factors make the collapse of the global financial system inevitable. One problem with capitalism is that it is not self-sufficient, but depends on the constant availability of new markets, forcing expansion by creating ever-increasing amounts of debt. We now have a globalized world market, so exploitation of new territories can no longer take place. As Naomi Klein analyzed in *The Shock Doctrine*, this led to a policy of "disaster capitalism," where cataclysms like hurricanes and terrorist acts were seized as opportunities to redevelop internal markets. Such a practice is inherently unsustainable.

Another crucial element that is rarely discussed in the media is the connection between the current financial meltdown and peak oil. Just as our debt-based economic system needed new markets to penetrate, it also required an ever-increasing supply of cheap energy to fuel its expansion. The decreasing supply of fossil fuels relative to global demand has brought the second law of thermodynamics into play, breaking the delusionary spell cast by the financier-sorcerers, who decoupled financial value from real value back in the early 1970s. When we consider the permanent reduction in the supply of cheap energy combined with the lack of new markets, it is obvious that the amassed debts will never be repaid.

Over the last decades, we have suffered through a massive transfer of financial assets from the poor and middle class to a tiny elite of the extremely wealthy. By a recent count, 691 billionaires had a combined net worth of $2.2 trillion. At the same time, an estimated 2.8 billion people survive on less than $2 a day. In the United States, less than 7,500 individuals control "almost three-quarters of the nation's industrial (nonfinancial) assets, almost two-thirds of all banking assets, and more than three-quarters of all insurance assets," according to Thomas Dye's *Who's Running America?* Members of this tiny group are found in the top echelons of our most exclusive law firms, investment banks, federal government posts, and military commands. Our current system is one of financial apartheid that rewards the most ecologically destructive and sociopathic behavior.

We face the possibility that money will soon lose its value as a medium of exchange. Given this, we will need to develop alternative ways of creating, exchanging, and sharing value. One interesting option is the potential for digital networks based on trust and reputation to replace many of the services now provided by our dollar-based economy. We may return to local currencies. Bernard Lietaer's proposal for a negative-interest currency linked to tangible assets that could act as a global trading medium should be taken seriously as an option.

In the near term, we face an increasingly turbulent and dangerous situation in the United States. Demagogues may attempt to control the situation with force. Some form of martial law is a real option. However, any attempt to impose martial law will only accelerate the collapse of our financial system. The ruling elite faces insoluble paradoxes. There is the potential for a triggering event similar to the nonviolent populist revolt that overcame the Soviet Union in 1989, surprising political experts and think tank analysts.

Despite the financial meltdown, the decline of resources, and the acceleration of climate change, we do not have to undergo a cataclysmic collapse. Through the new social technologies we have developed, we could quickly reorganize our society to allocate resources rationally. We could create collaborative networks that support a species-wide reeducation and the evolution of collective intelligence. We could shift from remote-control oligarchy to a true democracy, the "rule of all by all," constructing a society based on constant adaptation and resilient response.

THE PRESENT OF PRESENCE

Most people have not yet fully processed the magnitude of the economic crisis that will continue to deepen in the next years. Our lives may depend upon working through the causes and logical consequences of this disaster, which can be blamed on the greed and ineptitude of our ruling elite. The short-term prognosis is devastating. The hundreds of billions—potentially trillions—of dollars created by the U.S. government and Federal Reserve for bailouts should lead to hyperinflation, and a sharp rise in the price of basic goods. At the same time, some analysts are predicting the U.S. government will be insolvent within a few years and forced to declare bankruptcy.

One consequence of the credit freeze has been that many farmers around the world, who often live on narrow margins and depend upon loans to see them through the annual harvest, have not been able to get credit. This could lead to diminished production of food at a time when climate change is reducing the amount of arable land. Last year, there were already hunger riots in a number of countries, and by next summer, we may see famine on a larger scale.

Hunger has also become a hidden problem in the United States. While our economy contracts and layoffs as well as mass foreclosures continue, a large segment of our populace (who have no savings and much debt) has become a new pauper class. We have already seen over a million homes turned over to banks. One can only wonder where those people—and the millions more soon to join them—are going to end up.

Meanwhile, the turmoil in the markets will continue, potentially getting much worse. Apparently, hundreds of trillions of virtual dollars spin in the roulette machine of the derivatives market, which is beginning to disintegrate. The collapse of the housing market may be followed by mass waves of credit card defaults. Our economy was a house of cards, based on the extraordinary premise that ever-expanding debt was a desirable product, and it is now falling down upon us.

We are facing a period of great change and spiritual challenge. Those of us who have undergone a process of awakening and initiation during the last decades will be called upon to act as truth-tellers, leaders, and compassionate caretakers for the multitudes that have been duped and deluded by the system. We may have to abandon our comfort zones and personal ambitions to be of service to the situation as it unfolds.

In the time available to us before the situation becomes critical, priorities include strengthening local communities and disseminating techniques of self-sufficiency, such as getting many more people to grow their own food and produce their own energy. It is tragic that our mass media continue to act as a mechanism of distraction. The media could be used to explain to people how our world is changing, to teach them the basic life skills that we forfeited a few generations ago, and to imprint new behavior patterns based on sustainable life-ways. Perhaps public broadcasting, at least, can be repurposed for this necessary effort.

The partial nationalization of financial institutions around the world reveals the failure of capitalism—the end of capitalism in its old form. In the future, it should be obvious that capitalism was a transitional system for our human family. Capitalism meshed the world together through networks of trade and communication, while maintaining monstrous inequities and irrational misuse of resources.

The question that faces us now is, what comes after capitalism, and how do we get there? In the short term, we may see dangerous efforts at authoritarian control. The longer-term answer may be a collapse of centralized structures of authority and the blossoming of a new form of global direct democracy—what the anthropologist Pierre Clastres called "society without a state." By necessity, our future system will be collaborative rather than competitive.

If the crisis now confronting the human community is mishandled, vast populations will experience untold suffering and starvation in the next few years. If "we the people" can rise to the occasion, we may be able to radically change the direction of human society, along with the basic paradigms and underlying operating systems of our culture, in a rapid timeframe. This appears to be the message of many prophetic traditions—as the Hopi say, "We are the ones we have been waiting for"—which have anticipated this climactic passage in human affairs.

As we approach the holiday season and the Gregorian New Year, we can give thanks for having been born into this extraordinary, precious time. Our actions over the next few years could have tremendous consequences for humanity's future on this planet. At such a juncture, the best present we can give to the people around us is our authentic presence—our willingness to listen, learn, and remain open to transformation, as the pace of change quickens around us.

While exploring shamanism and non-ordinary states, I discovered the power of intention. According to the artist Ian Lungold, who lectured brilliantly about the Mayan Calendar before his untimely death a few years ago, the Maya believe that your intention is as essential to your ability to navigate reality as your position in time and space. If you don't know your intention, or if you are operating with the wrong intentions, you are always lost, and can only get more dissolute.

This idea becomes exquisitely clear during psychedelic journeys, when your state of mind gets intensified and projected kaleidoscopically all around you. As our contemporary world becomes more and more psychedelic, we are receiving harsh lessons in the power of intention, on a vast scale. Over the last decades, the international financial elite manipulated the markets to create obscene rewards for themselves at the expense of poor and middle-class people across the world. Using devious derivatives, cunning CDOS, and other trickery, they siphoned off ever larger portions of the surplus value created by the producers of real goods and services, contriving a debt-based economy that had to fall apart. Their own greed—such a meager, dull intent—has now blown up in their faces, annihilating, in slow motion, the corrupt system built to serve them.

Opportunities such as this one don't come along very often, and should be seized once they appear. When the institutions of society start to break down, as is happening now, it is a fantastic time for artists, visionaries, mad scientists, and seers to step forward and present a well-defined alternative. What is required is not some moderate proposal or incremental change, but a complete shift in values and goals, making a polar reversal of our basic paradigm. If our consumer-based, materialism-driven model of society is dissolving, what can we offer in its place? Why not begin with the most elevated intentions? Why not offer the most imaginatively fabulous systemic redesign?

The fall of capitalism and the crisis of the biosphere could induce mass despair and misery, or they could impel the creative adaptation and conscious evolution of the human species. We could attain a new level of wisdom and build a compassionate global society, in which resources are shared equitably while we devote ourselves to protecting threatened species and repairing damaged ecosystems. Considering the lightning-like speed of global communication and new social technologies, this change could happen with extraordinary speed.

To a very great extent, the possibilities that we choose to realize in the future will be a result of our individual and collective intention. For instance, if we maintain a Puritanical belief that work is somehow good in and of itself, then we will keep striving to create a society of full employment, even if those jobs become "green collar." A more radical viewpoint perceives most labor as something that could become essentially voluntary in the future. The proper use of technology could allow us to transition to a post-scarcity leisure society, where the global populace spends their time growing food, building community, making art, making love, learning new skills, and deepening their self-development through spiritual disciplines such as yoga, Tantra, shamanism, and meditation.

One common perspective is that the West and Islam are engaged in an intractable conflict of civilizations, where the hatred and terrorism can only get worse. Another viewpoint could envision the Judeo-Christian culture of the West finding common ground and reconciling with the esoteric core, the metaphysical purity, of the Islamic faith. It seems— to me anyway—that we could find solutions to all of the seemingly intractable problems of our time once we are ready to apply a different mind-set to them. As Einstein and others have noted, we don't solve problems through the type of thinking that created them, but dissolve them, when we reach a different level of consciousness.

We became so mired in our all-too-human world that we lost touch with the other, elder forms of sentience all around us. Along with delegates to the UN, perhaps we could train cadres of diplomats to negotiate with the vegetal, fungal, and microbial entities that sustain life on earth? The mycologist Paul Stamets proposes that we create a symbiosis with mushrooms to detoxify ecosystems and improve human health. The herbalist Morgan Brent believes psychoactive flora like ayahuasca and peyote are "teacher plants," sentient emissaries from superintelligent nature, trying to help the human species find its niche in the greater community of life. When we pull back to study the hapless and shameful activity of our species across the earth, these ideas do not seem very far-fetched.

In fact, the breakdown of our financial system has not altered the amount of tangible resources available on our planet. Rather than trying to rejigger an unjust debt-based system that artificially maintains inequity and scarcity, we could make a new start. We could develop a different intention for what we are supposed to be doing together on this swiftly tilting planet, and institute new social and economic infrastructures to support that intent.

THE AGE OF UNCERTAINTY

Recently, I have taken as my personal mantra the not very transcendent phrase, "I don't know." The list of things that I feel unsure about seems to be steadily increasing. For instance, I don't know if our solipsistic species will survive much longer, and sometimes I am not even sure how much I care. I don't know if Barack Obama is a warm-hearted leader who will unite people at a time of adversity, or the most brilliant puppet ever put forth by the New World Order conspirators, who, as Alex Jones suggests, may be plotting a program of rapid depopulation. I don't know if the increase in UFO sightings means we are approaching a benevolent contact experience or a horrific predatory ambush. I don't know if global warming is mainly caused by human action, or if it is part of a phase transition of the entire solar system, as the Russian scientist Alexey Dmitriev proposes.

I don't know if men and women should be monogamous or if it is better to be bonobo-like in one's erotic habits. I don't know if we will develop some type of new energy technology that will rescue us from peak oil, or if we are destined to see industrial civilization devolve and disintegrate as fossil fuel becomes scarce. I don't know whether to learn to grow food and harvest rainwater or to master some weird new esoteric discipline like Vortex Healing or Keylontic Science. I don't know if free will exists, or if we are conditioned robots, performing an illusory spectacle scripted by Hindu deities or dreamtime ancestors. I don't know if we should get rid of religions or create a really cool new one.

I don't know whether to stockpile gold or create an intentional community. I don't know whether to stay in Manhattan or head for the hills. I don't know whether we are approaching global enlightenment or regressing into barbarism. I don't know whether biotechnology and nanotechnology will fuse to give us immortal physical bodies or if we will all croak as our mistreated planet falls apart. I don't know if anything special will happen on December 21, 2012. I don't know if I should start a riot or throw a party. I don't know whether to panic or relax.

Something seems to be happening that is beyond my capacity to understand or articulate. I can only assume other people are feeling this way as well. We are witnessing the collapse of the old, rigidified structures, while the new hasn't come into realization yet—if there is going to be a new anything. A change seems to be happening at the level of logic, which is becoming less dualistic, less "either-or," and more binary, "both-and." Former diametric opposites are moving toward confluence, as well as dissonance, in various areas: like tweaked-out psychonauts, the physicists at CERN discuss opening portals into other dimensions. As the financial system evaporates, incredible new gizmos like Pandora and Cooliris spread freely on the Internet. Obama references Chicago 1968 in his acceptance speech at Grant Park, then hires as his economic advisers the guys who deregulated the banking system, causing the current disaster, under Clinton.

Reality is becoming more improvisational and up-tempo. Although I don't pretend to certainty about it, the ideas that José Argüelles, Terence McKenna, and others have proposed about time speeding up and going through ever faster fractal spirals of historical pantomime—including, alas, the mass suffering usually caused by historical convulsions— seem increasingly on the mark. If we are shifting away from dualistic separation and linear logic to a binary thought marked by polarities, this also suggests a shift from the modern historical perspective to a revived mythological consciousness. Like processes in the unconscious, myth resolves oppositions through symbol and image, without need of rational explanation. A society that reintegrates mythic thought at a deeper level of awareness will be able to handle seemingly contradictory perspectives without breaking down.

I don't know if we will live to see the birth of such a new worldview as part of a regenerated civilization, or if we only get to see the decline and fall of our current dinosaur. It does seem that ever-increasing numbers of people are done with it and ready to move on, but move on to what?

Some theorists propose that we have reached a point in evolution where we have the capacity to consciously co-create reality, and choose our own script for the future. Sometimes, this feels fuzzily plausible to me. On the other hand, our past actions and intentions have created the reality we experience now. It seems highly unlikely we can phase-shift to hyperspace, the fifth dimension, or whatever it is, until we have learned how to take proper care of this material world, and those who share it with us. Although maybe I am wrong and we will get a free pass. I just don't know.

AN EXTRAVAGANT HYPOTHESIS

As a hypothesis, I propose that humanity is currently undergoing a transition from the biological to the psychic phase of our species evolution. The inertia of physical forces, chemical processes, and cellular mechanisms, precisely coordinated over billions of years, has brought us to this make-or-break point. In order to continue our evolution, we need to reach a deeper level of species consciousness and self-awareness, transform our planetary culture and social systems so they serve the entire community of life, and integrate and anchor psychic capacities as part of a new paradigm and mythological substrate. This shift would also require a different approach to technological progress. We would use technology to create long-term benefit for people and planet, rather than short-sighted profits for individuals and corporations.

As individuals, we can choose to contribute to this process in essential ways. By shifting from passive spectators to active participants, we accept full responsibility for our own development and the unfolding of the whole. Currently, the first wave of individuals who are part of this tipping-point

phenomenon are learning to observe themselves as partici-
pators within the cosmos, and to act in our earthly realm
with impartiality and compassion.

According to this hypothesis, as this level of presence
crystallizes among the few, it will become increasingly
available to wider circles of humanity, until it encompasses
the entirety. We will supersede the confusion and destruction caused by the modern process of individuation by
establishing new models of inclusive collaboration. As one
aspect of this phase shift in consciousness, we will see a
shift from hierarchic to holarchic models of social organization, and the melding of masculine rationality with
feminine intuition. The form of the modern nation-state,
obsessed with defending its own insecure boundaries, will
be outmoded by a global direct democracy in which local
communities realize themselves as fractal expressions of
the greater hologram, like healthy cells of the planetary
organism.

Many mystical traditions propose that what we experience as reality is actually a kind of waking dream, projected from an infinite source of consciousness. According
to this hypothesis, each of us can identify with our personal ego—the dream character in the dream play—or
switch our center of identification to the projecting source.
While the ego is trapped in limitation, the projecting
source is infinite and free. Given the right marketing campaign, the awareness of our connection with this infinite

creative source could permeate the global mind in the same way a new pop song or advertising jingle insinuates itself into the collective subconscious.

The uncertainty that many of us feel right now is, in itself, part of this transitional process. Whether we like it or not, the responsibility for the future of the species has now been placed in our hands. If we don't answer this call, our species will experience rapidly intensifying cataclysms as the negative feedback loops of climate change, species extinction, resource depletion, fundamentalist violence, and overpopulation create hell on earth, perhaps leading to our own extinction.

As I have discussed in previous works, there are good reasons to think that the positive feedback loops could also come together and self-reinforce to create a successful outcome—what Buckminster Fuller described as a "win-win" situation for global humanity. It appears that successive transformations of human civilization happen at exponentially faster rates of linear time: While the Agricultural Revolution took thousands of years, the Industrial Age took under two hundred years, and the Knowledge or Information Age required only a few decades. By this model, as Peter Russell has suggested, the next revolution in human society could happen in two or three years. This would be a revolution of wisdom, of consciousness, that could, potentially, open the gates to the psychic phase of our development.

More and more people appear to be experiencing psychic phenomena—synchronicities, intuitive realizations, telepathic episodes, and even occasional phenomena such as sudden manifestations or telekinesis. Anecdotally, I also encounter many people now undergoing classic kundalini experiences, which were once extremely rare. A number of scientists have proposed that the solar system and the earth are undergoing a transition to a higher energy state. The level of electromagnetic activity may be increasing on our planet, accelerating and intensifying our psychic evolution. We may find that there is a nondual relationship between changes in our lives on earth and processes happening throughout our solar system and the galaxy.

The correlations between ancient mystical traditions and the discoveries of quantum physics and other modern scientific disciplines could be firmly established, and presented in popular media so that they become socially accepted. The empirical tools of modern science could be repurposed to facilitate the development of psychic awareness, while our communications technologies transmit a new understanding around the planet in an extremely concentrated timeframe. At the same time, we could use the mass media and the Internet to disseminate the best techniques for growing food locally, for producing renewable energies, for reinventing industries and creating complementary currencies, and so on.

Of course, I don't know if this hypothetical outcome will come to pass. However, I see no reason why it couldn't. The tools are there for us. All that is required is the individual and collective will to make use of them.

For the most part, the mainstream media and federal government still treat the economic collapse as something that can be fixed, so that economic growth can resume in a few years. Some commentators are beginning to realize that our meltdown represents a deeper and more permanent paradigm shift. The physical environment can no longer withstand the assaults of our industrial culture. We are experiencing a termination of capitalism as we have known it, a shutdown recently dubbed "The Great Disruption" by Thomas Friedman, in *The New York Times*. Until recently a leading cheerleader for Neoliberal globalization, Friedman has come to the late realization that "the whole growth model we created over the last fifty years is simply unsustainable economically and ecologically and that 2008 was when we hit the wall." The longer the general population is allowed to remain in denial about what is happening, the more dire the probable consequences, such as widespread famine, civil unrest, and a disintegration of basic services.

The truth is that we need to make a deep and rapid change in our current social systems and in the underlying models and ideals of our society. It is highly unlikely that those who have been part of the power structure, whether within government or the mainstream media, possess the necessary will, vision, or inspiration to make this happen. Also, when we consider their self-serving support for a delusional model of infinite growth on a finite planet, ignoring all evidence to the contrary, our mainstream pundits and politicos have clearly forfeited any claim to authority, and should never be trusted again.

Many elements of an alternative paradigm, a participatory model in which power is restored to local communities, have been developed over the last decades. The Transition Town model from the UK is one approach to supporting communities as they move toward resilience and self-reliance. Every year, the Bioneers Conference presents a number of extraordinary initiatives, and its Web site maintains an archive of these projects, from bioremediation to complementary currencies, that could be rapidly scaled up once the collective will is mobilized. The nonprofit organization Pro-Natura has developed an alfalfa leaf extract that can fulfill a person's annual nutritive needs for a negligible sum—and many other innovative scientists and activist groups hold crucial pieces of the new puzzle we need to assemble quickly.

What blocks real efforts at social transformation is the current level of human consciousness. The Italian political philosopher Antonio Negri has noted that the most important form of production in our post-industrial culture is the "production of subjectivity"—our media and education systems have mechanically imprinted a certain level of awareness onto the masses, a passive, consumer consciousness. People have not been encouraged to think or to act for themselves. Now, their very survival may depend upon learning these unfamiliar skills.

Since I comprehended the inescapable crisis heading our way, I have been working with friends and collaborators to envision and enact solutions. We saw the need for an alternative social network and media that could integrate many aspects of the new paradigm while providing a scaffold for a large-scale process of social transformation. Facebook and MySpace reveal the extraordinary power of social networks to reach an enormous audience, but they mainly provide a place for people to display and distract themselves in new ways. Most popular social networks are designed to support what media critic Thomas de Zengotita has called the "flattered self," constantly craving attention. The overriding purpose of these networks is to make a profit for corporations.

We have just launched Evolver (evolver.net), an independent social network, built on open-source software, that is designed to support collaboration between individuals and groups, to reinvigorate civil society, and to engage people in the process of transforming their own consciousness and their local communities. While we still use many of the standard social networking tools, we have shifted the focus to members' missions and projects. We have also created an internal rating system for members to vote on the initiatives presented by other members, so that the best ideas in every area will rise to the top and gain more attention. Our plan is to facilitate a network of local groups, across the United States and coordinated globally, that meet in person and engage in immediate actions to change their world.

Years ago, Barbara Marx Hubbard wrote, "If the positive innovations connect exponentially before the massive breakdowns reinforce one another, the system can repattern itself to a higher order of consciousness and freedom without the predicted economic, environmental, or social collapse." We are quickly approaching the critical threshold where breakdown or breakthrough becomes inevitable. I don't know if Evolver will reach mass popularity as a tool to bring about this repatterning. Of course, I hope this is the case. In the guise of a for-profit company, we seek to create something akin to a social utility. At a turbulent time when nobody knows what is going to happen next, it feels good, at least, to have launched something into the world that can help to reawaken and restore civil society.

SATELLITE OF LOVE: THOUGHTS
ON THE NORWAY SPIRAL

On December 9, 2009, a startling event took place over the early morning sky in Norway: a perfect white spiral that emanated a spinning bright blue beam before vanishing into a black circular hole. The numinous spectacle, witnessed by thousands of people across the country, was extensively documented in photographs and videos. By the next afternoon, the authorities had issued a conventional explanation through the media, claiming that this unusual apparition was a failed Russian missile test.

Over the next weeks, mystics, skeptics, Fortean investigators, Pleiadian channels, and aeronautic engineers debated the event and the explanation offered for it across the Internet. Following these debates, many people—myself among them—found the official story to be unsatisfying. Footage of failed rockets and botched missile launches tend to have an uneven, sputtering trajectory. The Norway spiral, on the other hand, was unerringly precise and flawlessly geometric. We also learned that the Norway spiral was not an entirely isolated event. Over the last few years, identical inexplicable phenomena have been filmed in other parts of the world, including China and South America.

The Norway spiral seemed impeccably timed. The apparition shone forth just a few hours before President Obama accepted the Nobel Peace Prize in Oslo. In his unusual speech, Obama defended the idea of a "just war," and made no commitment to bring home the hundreds of thousands of U.S. troops and private mercenaries stationed across Afghanistan and Iraq. The spiral also coincided with the Copenhagen Climate Conference, a notable fiasco where international leaders failed to resolve the gridlock over laissez-faire policies on climate change, at a time when low-lying island nations are beginning to disappear beneath the waves.

If the spiral was not a missile that sputtered out, some commentators have theorized, it was a deliberate demonstration of a secret military technology, perhaps related to the HAARP Project. However, it is unclear what kind of message would have been conveyed by such a display. Another hypothesis is that the Norway spiral was indeed a communication, but one with a nonhuman or extraterrestrial origin. Personally, I find myself open to that theory based on my past research on the crop circles. In *2012: The Return of Quetzalcoatl*, I explored the phenomenon of the crop circles—geometrical patterns, often of an extraordinary complexity and virtuosity—that appear each summer in wheat fields around the world, but most dramatically in southern England, in the stone circle–riddled area of Wiltshire. I spent several years studying the crop formations that appear each year, and ended up convinced that they could not be entirely explained away as a hoax, art project, or human-made effort. The phenomenon, as a whole, seemed to be a kind of primer, a method for teaching certain ideas and principles, over time. I proposed that through the crop circles, we received lessons about fundamental principles of sacred geometry and insights into the nature of consciousness. The crop circles suggest that it is our level of consciousness that determines the value of any phenomena we experience, and even shapes what phenomena we perceive.

The crop circles, like the Norway spiral, seem an interactive phenomenon—an interaction, perhaps, between our human minds and a form of consciousness and intelligence that is significantly beyond our current evolutionary stage. One piece of good news, if we are willing to consider the crop circles and the Norway spiral as messages or teachings, is that we are, at the very least, being honored with conversation. For something to register as communication, rather than being immediately dismissed as meaningless noise, there needs to be a transmitter and a receiver, allowing for interaction between two parties.

When I first saw the spiral, I felt intuitively that the spectacle was intentionally created to help open human consciousness, at a time of increasing confusion and crisis here on earth. Albert Einstein and other great thinkers have noted that problems—like war, perhaps, or climate change—cannot be solved by the same level of consciousness that created them. However, it is possible that they can be resolved, or superseded, if consciousness jumps to a different level, encompassing a wider context and a deeper perception. Following the works of the Russian scientist Alexey Dmitriev and others, it is conceivable that an event like the Norway spiral could be a plasma phenomenon—plasma that is artificially induced and intelligently guided. The apparition shares many characteristics with the crop circles that appear each summer, including their maddening daimonic quality, which makes it difficult if not impossible to anchor any singular cause or mechanism.

Because of my research into indigenous myth, the Norway spiral reminded me of a sign foretold by the oral prophecy of the Hopi. The Hopi expect an apparition in the sky, called the Blue Star Kachina, to appear at the end of our current Fourth World, as we cross the threshold into the Fifth. This prophecy has been integrated into the global culture of New Age spirituality, becoming one archetypal element in the collective psychic field. Therefore, if the spiral is in some sense an interactive communication between the human mind and the consciousness of an "other," the designer may have drawn upon this archetype or expectation in spraying this luminous graffiti across the Scandinavian sky.

The psychoanalyst Carl Jung wrote about the flying

saucer phenomenon in the 1950s, and proposed that whatever tangible reality the UFOs had, the UFO also represents an archetypal process that continues to mature within the individual and collective human psyche. The round shape of the saucers, for Jung, symbolized psychic wholeness, the alchemical completion of the "Great Work" in the integration of conscious and unconscious aspects of the Psyche. Jung noted that the movement toward psychic wholeness takes the form of a spiral that moves around the center, inexorably closer to it with each passage. The Norway spiral seemed to reference this process in its rapid blossoming across the sky.

It is quite possible that the Norway spiral was either a botched attempt to launch some new form of military technology, or a successful effort to demonstrate a new capacity now possessed by some government. It is also possible that the spiral is a message from the collective psyche and/or the mind of an other—perhaps an invitation to explore the indeterminate nature of the psyche, perhaps an indication that the earth and its human inhabitants have reached the cusp of an inescapable process that will transmute or transform us into something extremely different from what we have been until now. While much of my work over the last years has been an effort to understand the process of change or transmutation that I believe to be under way, I still find myself challenged and even cowed by it.

The process we have entered does seem like a spiral or vortex that is sucking our world toward a center point, whether we consciously desire it or not. The analytical tools of the mind seem increasingly limited as we approach the center point. When we examine the decimation caused to the biosphere by human tampering or the volatile changes to the activities of the sun and other planets throughout the solar system that our satellites can measure, it seems we have no choice but to surrender to what is unfolding, to open our hearts to it. Rather than fear it, we can trust that the apparently intensifying chaos is not simply drawing us toward dissolution, but will ultimately bring our human world into a new harmonic balance, unveiling a deeper order.

Like the crop circles, the Norway spiral suggests there are more advanced levels of consciousness—galactic federations, perhaps—hovering in the wings, probably keeping watch over us. Considering the rapid progress humanity experienced in a mere two hundred years of technological development, I find it totally sensible to expect that any form of conscious species that survives 1,000 or 100,000 or a million years beyond the stage we have reached would have developed levels of technology, and I suspect psychic technologies, far beyond anything we imagine. They would probably have a vested interest in seeing us prosper, as more forms of embodied consciousness can only make an evolving multiverse a more beautiful and entertaining place.

Outside of the science fiction genre, our culture has not deeply explored the possibility that contact and communion with other levels of galactic intelligence may have happened frequently across human history. Those beings that are commonly considered "angels"—as well as the otherworldly visitors known from folktales around the world—could reflect a secret history of communication between humanity and the other dimensions of consciousness that may populate the cosmos. This area of study is not encouraged or even generally permitted in universities, leaving it up to outsiders like Zecharia Sitchin, Erich von Däniken, and José Argüelles to research it.

Modern writers who explore this idea are marginalized and consigned to the New Age fringe. When I read their work, it is often difficult to isolate what has a legitimate basis, and what reveals their psychological projection onto the material. Authors David Icke and Michael Tsarion, for example, propose that the earth is under a type of quarantine. They offer forceful, if sketchy, arguments that our planet is currently ruled by an extraterrestrial race they characterize as "reptilian." Icke and Tsarion believe that this control group continues to dominate through genetic "bloodlines" that can be traced back to the royal families of Europe. This entire complex of thought is a contemporary upgrade of Gnostic cosmology, which sees our world governed by malevolent off-planet entities that the Gnostics called "Archons." However, to say that it updates Gnostic mythology does not, in itself, validate or invalidate their ideas.

In *The Philosopher's Secret Fire*, Patrick Harpur interrogates the literalism of our modern worldview, which is almost impossible for us to escape. Harpur argues that traditional cultures based on a mythological understanding of reality were not caught in this literal bind—that they understood that reality could always and in any case be otherwise, that myth was necessary as a way to shape the world into a form that we can share. "We cannot see the world except through some perspective or imaginative framework—in short, some myth," Harpur writes. "Indeed, the world we see is the myth we are in."

Harpur slyly proposes that "history is the mythological variant we have chosen to take literally." A story, a myth, or a historical narrative is like a warm coat we weave around us for protection and comfort. Any story we construct, whether an Eskimo's folktale or the most up-to-date explanations offered by science, is a limit we define, and can also become a straitjacket that constricts us. We cannot live without telling myths, and we become the myth that we tell.

Up until now, efforts to codify various concepts about extraterrestrial visitors into a coherent understanding have tended to founder, often leading to unappealing literalism or convolutions that verge on psychosis. As one example of the latter, Voyagers is a series of books by Ashayana Deane, a channel who claims to speak for the Guardian Alliance, a benevolent federation of extraterrestrial and hyperdimensional civilizations. The Voyagers books propose that our lives are stretched between numerous dimensions and timelines, multiple "harmonic universes" that are parallel yet contingent upon each other. Certain aliens can make "holographic inserts" into our seemingly solid-state reality that become tangible events we collectively experience, shifting history onto different timelines. Deane's books are voluminous with detail, and the galactic history they recount is difficult to absorb, unfathomably far-fetched, and exuberantly entertaining. As you evolve, Deane writes, "you will train your consciousness to move backward and forward in time, to re-create undesired events and redesign more desirable outcomes." For Deane and many other mediums, the world is literally a dream play, a thought projection that can be remolded by consciousness at any time. In works like Deane's, we see a new mythology weaving together, where the archaic other world of ancient myth and antique fairy tale melds with a galactic saga of super-advanced aliens, forming a new amalgam.

If literalism is, in itself, a limit to be superseded, how will we find a shared language to integrate the numinous experiences of other levels and forms of consciousness, reported by so many people, in such varied circumstances? Perhaps this is a task for the next age that cultures like the Hopi and Maya appear to have anticipated through their prophecies.

Was the Norway spiral misfired technology or intergalactic transmission? Did it represent a new intensity of psychic energy entering our world, penetrating from thought into material form? Is it conceivable that the Norway spiral, like a sudden bolt of lightning, was intended to be a shock of illumination, shaking humanity from our long psychic slumber, awakening us into a deeper level of the cosmic play?

Only you can decide.

MY JOURNEY INTO THE
EVOLVER SOCIAL MOVEMENT

The launch of the Evolver Social Movement has been a process fraught with anxiety and propelled by enthusiasm. At this critical juncture in the life of our project, I find myself wanting to review the sequence of events that led to this point. What follows is a look back into the remote past, and then a consideration of what we are doing now, and what may lie ahead.

I started the first version of Evolver about five years ago, with a company in Venice, California. One of the investors in that company e-mailed me after reading a few of my columns for a Los Angeles–based alt-culture monthly. Together, we developed a model for a new company, the Evolver Project, combining a membership program with media, including a print magazine, Evolver. I spent a year and a half involved in that effort before the company fell apart.

Before I was tapped for that first Evolver attempt, I was truly a rube when it came to business. I was writing my books and living like a grumpy urban hermit in New York, feeling exiled from the mainstream due to my fascination with psychedelics, prophecy, and other areas of marginal weirdness. During the brief poignant life of the Evolver Project, I received brutal lessons in how not to run a company, as I watched resources get spent before we had a defined product or even a way of making revenue. This was difficult for me, as I tend to be frugal where possible, having learned to stretch out small publishing advances over long fallow periods.

Toward the end of that first effort, I brought Ken Jordan on board. Ken was one of my closest friends. He worked in publishing (following in the footsteps of his father, Fred Jordan, publisher of Grove Press and the *Evergreen Review*), but didn't like the increasingly corporate, cookie-cutter direction that publishing had taken. I suggested that he seek a job in the then emergent Web world and introduced him to friends of mine launching Sonic.net, a music Web site, eventually bought by MTV. Later on, Ken joined up with Planetwork, a nonprofit think tank started by West Coast visionary Jim Fournier, to look at ways that Internet tools could be used to advance progressive goals. Ken helped develop a major Planetwork paper on the concept of the Augmented Social Network, the ASN.

The essential problem that Ken's Planetwork group identified was that Internet users lacked a secure, centralized place to hold their identity. The way the Net is now organized, we carom between different "walled silos" that take our data and make use of it or sell it, without our knowledge. The ASN paper proposed the need for a new layer of the Internet, where personal identity information and transactions would be stored in one place, for the user's benefit. Users would then choose what parts of their profile to reveal to any group or organization they visited. This would also allow for different organizations or companies to collaborate effectively, as their users could let them know how they were connected with other groups. Today, different NGOs reduplicate effort and even compete against each other for the same members and sponsors, with little coordination, fighting for scarce resources.

Ken had to explain the ASN ideas to me again and again, for over a year, before I finally understood what I now consider to be their immense importance (some similar ideas have been implemented, such as Open ID, but these do not approach the scope of the ASN vision). It sounds quite dry at first, but if you spend time studying the issue, I think you will find that the lack of a way for people to maintain their own identity and control their own data is a massive problem, one that thwarts the healthy development of civil society.

I brought Ken into Evolver because I saw the opportunity to implement his ASN vision through our model of building a membership card program for the "cultural creatives," the most progressive and ecologically aware subset of U.S. consumers. We intended to build a user-centered profile system that integrated the latest aspects of this developing protocol. Unfortunately, as the clock ran out on that first effort, which had been renamed EVO, it did not happen.

In the wake of the collapse of EVO, Ken and I still wanted to work together. Meeting at coffee shops in the East Village, we considered what we could start for basically no money, which is all we had. I had been running a discussion board for *Breaking Open the Head*, my first book on psychedelic shamanism, on the Web. From the impassioned personal and philosophical exchanges on that forum, I knew there was a vast amount of extraordinary material, important ideas, and visionary testimonies that needed a professional media presence to reach beyond a small group and influence the broader cultural debate. Ken was able to get Civic Actions to build the platform for Reality Sandwich in exchange for some equity in our company.

I always had an innate tendency to start magazines. In high school I edited our literary journal, *Chimera*. In college, my friends and I created our own literary journal, *Planetarium Station*, which we xeroxed and then bound together. We featured some amazing writers who later went on to major careers, including Mark Amerika and the poet Anne Carson.

After dropping out of Wesleyan University in Connecticut, I launched a career in commercial art and lifestyle magazines, working as an intern at *Art & Auction*, then as an assistant and associate editor at *Fame* (short-lived and unlamented) and *Connoisseur* (a century-old Hearst magazine that went belly-up after my first year there). At the same time, I made friends with a tall, charismatic young fiction writer, Thomas Beller. Together we launched the literary magazine *Open City*, eventually finding a publisher in Rob Bingham, a short story writer and heir to a southern newspaper fortune.

Through *Open City*, we made a decadent, somewhat glamorous, scene, throwing parties in nightclubs and art galleries and at Rob's huge loft in Tribeca. Various celebs passed through—such as Chloë Sevigny, Evan Dando, Parker Posey—and we were written up in fashion magazines and gossip columns. I no longer worked full-time and I spent altogether too much time at Rob's loft playing pool and lounging about. While my pool game improved, my life stagnated. I was working on fiction but experiencing little success with it, while I wrote freelance magazine articles to make a sort of living. I began to feel increasingly alienated and depressed—as described in my books. Eventually I plunged into a massive spiritual crisis and existential emergency, often feeling I was on the verge of going insane.

I simply couldn't understand the point of all of our frantic activity since we lived in a nihilistic universe, accidentally created by swirling gasses and particles, where death returned us to an absolute void. In my social set at that time, to open up big philosophical questions about the nature of reality and the soul was only to invite sarcasm and hipster dismissal. My friends conceived literature as a way of seeking the proper pose or stance in relationship to a world that had no meaning outside of one's personal style and ability to see it with a perfectly jaundiced eye and finely turned phrases pitched just right.

I became interested in psychedelics as a way out of my spiritual crisis, recalling early college trips that had opened my eyes to other levels or layers of reality. These substances were scorned by my peers, but I became fascinated by them again. I went to Gabon for a ritual using iboga, becoming a Bwiti, an initiate. I wrote about ayahuasca and LSD psychoanalyst Stanislav Grof for *The Village Voice*. As I was exploring this area, Rob, our publisher, was found dead of a heroin overdose in his loft, with the page proofs of his first novel spread across the desk in his extraordinarily chaotic office.

I had already begun to distance myself from the literary culture of my peers, but Rob's death pushed me further away. I increasingly felt that most current literature as well as much contemporary art had become a distraction mechanism and ego trip, offering a way of contemplating the degraded and fragmented state of our world from a safe distance instead of making active efforts to change it. Eventually, I bowed out of *Open City*, which was continued after Rob's death by his family out of a desire to honor his memory and support his legacy. While *Open City* still publishes today, I have not been involved in many years. Still I believe the enterprise has validity, as it has given many writers their first publications, launching a number of careers.

Over the next six or so years, I published my first two books, *Breaking Open the Head* in 2002 and *2012: The Return of Quetzalcoatl* in 2006. I then resumed my peculiarly inveterate habit of launching new magazines with *Reality Sandwich* in 2007. Both Ken and I were astounded by the flood of content that was quickly offered to us for *Reality Sandwich*, much of it of a shockingly high quality. We soon realized we had created something with a life of its own—a nexus where psychedelic culture and mainstream social and environmental thought could intersect, a cultural dialogue that needed to take place. Some of our features received hundreds of comments, and the commentators often expressed a yearning to find others living near them who shared similar interests.

This project has flowed organically since we launched. Once we saw the demand, we decided to build a social network to bring together our growing community. On modest initial investments, we launched Evolver.net, using Drupal, an open-source publishing platform. The shift from simply running another social network in virtual space to using Evolver.net as a hub for organizing off-line real-world communities also happened naturally: Jonathan Phillips—one of the four people who initially founded the company along with Ken, myself, and Michael Robinson, our brilliant creative director—has a strong background in community organizing. He began, quite naturally, to guide groups coming together in other cities as well as in the United States. We realized that developing these nascent connections into vibrant communities was the central mission of our project.

Even in this early and challenging stage, we have learned that the merging of professional online media with a social network that supports the growth of off-line communities—moving from virtual to visceral—is an extremely powerful innovation. As a new form of "interdependent media," we can continually offer new tools and ideas for our growing community to explore, then report on their discoveries through articles and videos. We live at a time when the financial system and other forms of social infrastructure are breaking down and the future looks increasingly uncertain for many.

As a recent issue of *Time* magazine predicts, the new ten-year trend is "The Dropout Economy," where young people are forced to explore radical alternatives as work disappears and the financial burden becomes intolerable: "As conventional high schools and colleges prepare the next generation for jobs that won't exist, we're on the cusp of a dropout revolution, one that will spark an era of experimentation in new ways to learn and new ways to live." *Time*'s forecast could be read as a desperate plea that young people, instead of rising up in fury against the older generation that depleted the planet's resources at their expense, will make virtue out of necessity: "Faced with the burden of financing the decades-long retirement of aging boomers, many of the young embrace a new underground economy, a largely untaxed archipelago of communes, co-ops, and kibbutzim that passively resist the power of the granny state while building their own little utopias." Ahead of the curve, we developed *Reality Sandwich* and Evolver to serve and support these emergent, now inevitable, circumstances.

We are delighted with the growth of Evolver, and gratified by the intense loyalty and enthusiasm it continues to elicit. The main thing holding us back has been a stubborn lack of operating capital. We have started a number of projects and been forced to put them aside. We developed the Evolver Exchange, a marketplace platform for Evolvers to sell and trade their goods and services, as well as featuring companies that accord with our community's values. Due to lack of funds, we couldn't launch this site. We had the opportunity to shoot using green screen, recording the silhouettes of a professional dance troupe, for an Evolver.net promo video. Unfortunately, we never had the resources for postproduction. We want to redesign and overhaul Evolver.net, adding new features and making it far more user-friendly, augmenting its ability to function as a tool for civil society. We never had a marketing budget for *Reality Sandwich*, which now reaches more than 100,000 readers per month on its own merit. I could easily list another ten or twenty deserving projects that we have not been able to fund up to this point, tools that would help our community as well as create revenue for the project.

In the past, a sizable pool of investors understood that the bottom line was not the only determining factor in deciding whether certain projects got a legitimate chance to succeed. These people would patronize the arts, endow a magazine, and support other types of cultural ventures and social initiatives. They believed that championing a vision or fighting for a cause was a way of creating value—what the sociologist Pierre Bourdieu called "culture capital"—and was also a form of reward. This type of patronage still exists but has become rare. Today, socially progressive investors also confront a bewildering blizzard of possibly promising projects that incessantly seek their support. Given so many options, they find it difficult to determine how to use resources most effectively.

While independent media ventures like Grove Press or *The Village Voice* were given many years of support before they broke even, today most independent media start-ups are quickly shut down if they don't measure up to the high yields produced by bottom-line-oriented companies. Only media that panders to a low common denominator have a chance to succeed in this financial climate. Evolver has been extremely lucky to find a handful of brave and visionary investors who saw the value in our project, and provided the capital that got us to this point. Unfortunately, we have not found enough capital to give us a lead time of even six months to a year—enough of a cushion to develop and promote projects that generate reliable revenue, at a time when traditional sources such as advertising have evaporated. We have, therefore, found ourselves in a constant semi-starvation mode of scrambling for bare resources. I feel sad as well as frustrated when I compare Evolver's situation to that of corporate media conglomerates that seem to cater to the interests of the military-industrial complex, as well as so many companies that have deep pockets to produce, promote, and distribute the products of Third World sweatshops, dangerous chemicals, or industrialized food that is detrimental to human health and the biosphere.

Beyond all commercial incentives, writing my previous book, *2012: The Return of Quetzalcoatl,* convinced me that this is a time of intense transition—that humanity will either evolve our consciousness and take individual and eventually species-wide responsibility for our effects on the planet, or we won't have much future here. The Evolver Social Movement is the best vehicle I have been able to conceive, along with my Evolver cohorts, to hasten this transformation, by helping to build a viable alternative culture in local communities, and by producing media that spread the word. Media shape the consciousness of the masses, and unless we can transmit a different set of messages through the mainstream, it will be extremely difficult to change our society's destructive habits.

Vast multitudes are trapped in the matrix—our culture's constrained system of rewards and punishments—and incapable of exploring what might lie beyond it. In New York City, most people do not conceive that the hyper-consumerist and self-centered lifestyle to which they are accustomed will soon be untenable. In all likelihood, massive change will come about through a combination of factors that include a much deeper crash of the economic system, shortages of fossil fuels and other necessities, an intensifying series of disasters like the earthquakes that recently wracked Haiti and Chile, and civil unrest and tax rebellion as people understand there can be no return to "normal" growth, as we have hit the resource limits on the biosphere. I am pretty sure this will be the case at any rate—although, admittedly, I don't know for certain. It is possible that I am biased, as I innately disagree with many aspects of our society. However, I do feel that an impartial overview of the available data leads to this conclusion, as many people, and even *Time* magazine, are now realizing.

I look forward to a transformation of our culture and a deep shift in our system of values. Personally, I hope this happens through a global awakening of consciousness rather than a series of catastrophes. I anticipate we may have both for a while—much like the violent convulsions that accompany a birthing process.

Recently, I held a public dialogue with the great filmmaker Abel Ferrara, known for dark underworld fables like *King of New York* and *Bad Lieutenant*, at Collective Hardware on the Bowery. Ferrara sees that our society has become untenable and unsustainable. Yet he seemed unable to recognize that this situation might require an active rather than reactive response—that we actually need to build the scaffold for the new society and value system while the old one melts down. I find that most people from the older generation share this blind spot. Many artists embrace the culture's destructive tendencies, even glamorizing the dysfunctional characters who emerge from our cynical doom-spiral state. We tend to dwell upon the muck, rather than use art to envision and inspire the way out of it.

We started Evolver and *Reality Sandwich* because we felt the real need for "interdependent media" that express both a practical and visionary alternative. As Buckminster Fuller noted, we have the capacity to redesign society, using resources far more efficiently, elevating human consciousness, aligning with the biosphere, and creating a "win-win" scenario for humanity—but most people have no idea this is possible. At the moment, we are coming close to failing what Fuller called our final exam as a species, "to take on the responsibility we've been designed to be entrusted with."

The idea to launch the Evolver Social Movement by going to our community and asking them to support what we already do, instead of trying to create a new project to generate revenue, came from one of our investors. Our first reaction was to reject this proposal. It was so simple that it seemed counterintuitive. Given a few days to think on it, we realized this was, actually, the natural and authentic approach. By becoming a member of the Evolver Social

Movement, you directly support alternative media that present radical and transformative ideas, and help develop our network of local communities in the United States and abroad.

Since investment is scarce while advertising revenues have dried up, our best hope for Evolver is to appeal directly to you. We ask that you consider what our project provides, and decide if it is in your best interests to see it flourish and thrive. If you see the value in it, we hope you will join and contribute. This is an elegant, egalitarian, grassroots solution. We are letting the people choose. And if you do choose to support Evolver.net, we intend to solicit your participation at a deeper level as the project goes forward.

To a certain extent, I enjoy salesmanship, marketing, and promotion. When *2012: The Return of Quetzalcoatl* was published, I relentlessly pushed the publicity department to pursue every lead I could uncover. I intend to be equally relentless about pushing the Evolver Social Movement over the next few months. I will probably bore, annoy, and irritate many people along the way. But I am used to that. Some people may feel that we have compromised or betrayed their trust. At this point, I don't mind if we lose the uncommitted segment of our community, at least for a while, as we make our needs and priorities clear. While I am sympathetic to the anticapitalist reactions we get from some people, they simply don't leave room for Evolver to survive. Rather than entirely dropping out or abandoning the system, we have no choice but to make use of it, as long as it lasts.

If the Evolver Social Movement flourishes, we can pursue a number of hopefully useful goals. I admit, ironically, that I am one of the world's worst joiners. I almost never join any type of group, affiliation, or association, and will go out of my way to avoid doing so, no matter what difficulties it creates. Launching the ESM, I am reminded of Groucho Marx's quip that he would never belong to any club that would have him as a member. I have made an exception in this case, and can only hope others will do the same.

Growing up in New York City, I always felt totally alienated from community and from politics. While I marched in some protests, including those against the Iraq War, I often wondered why I bothered. There are times when protest is necessary. However, more and more people are realizing that you can never change anything by opposing it or fighting against it—often, you end up feeding it energy. The only way to change a bad situation is to build the thing that is good, that will replace the old corrupt system.

For the most part, we lack forums where people can learn about what is happening, and organize around the critical issues of our time. The Evolver Regionals can help provide this. Our civil society is a scarecrow of a true democratic body, with most people pacified, distracted, and ignorant. Our financial system is an extraordinary sorceror's instrument designed to expropriate value from poor and middle-class people and funnel the wealth to an elite class of financial capitalists and speculators. This process has actually become far more intense in recent years, reaching astonishingly surrealist levels. The mass media keep people in a state of anxiety and distraction, while our financial institutions entangle people in debt and obligation. While a few live high on the hog, most people face an ever more uncertain and impoverished future.

As members of this society, we collude in our government's ruinous policies if we do not come together to bring an end to them. To take one example, the United States is still engaged in two horrific wars, with over a million Iraqi civilians dead as a result of the campaign in Iraq, for which we still have no legitimate justification. In actual fact, our social institutions are currently in the throes of a deep legitimization crisis. Overwhelming force, in itself, does not justify illegal and immoral activities. Given no obvious alternative, people allow themselves to be distracted and deluded by meaningless infotainment. The only way we can build a more resilient and sustaining world is by designing new social infrastructure that organizes and activates the dormant genius of civil society.

Reality Sandwich and Evolver.net are already a hub for alternative news and views, for essays and articles exploring the radical edge of human thought. Given your support, we can develop more powerful and professional media that expose and investigate, incite and inspire. At the same time, the Evolver Social Movement builds a scaffold for local communities to mesh visionary ideals with practical solutions. In the future, these communities can take a united stand on issues our global community deems to be critical. We believe the Evolver Social Movement shows a possible path forward, a way we can find each other, then use our cunning and creativity to reinvent a society whose destructive activities threaten the future of this world. Considering all of this, I hope you will decide to join forces with us in this social experiment—or, to use a term from the artist Joseph Beuys, "social sculpture"—and participate in ways that you find inspiring and that bring you joy.

THE NEED TO BELIEVE

When my father died in the summer of 2000, he left behind hundreds of paintings and sculptures in his rent-controlled loft on Greene Street—the relics of a lifelong investigation. The work ranged from severe wooden constructions made in the 1960s to woozy zigzags created out of plaster; from icon-sized images to rolled-up canvases of vast dimensions. My father's art went ignored, essentially unseen, during his lifetime. There were no career retrospectives, no museum shows, no fanfare. His artist friends were his central audience.

In the aftermath of his life, I found myself compelled to fight his battle for him: I remained convinced that my father's art counts as late-breaking news from the last century. The work he left behind is probing and profound, abject and obstinate, luminous and eerie, eccentric yet true to its own inner logic. It revels in metaphysical doubt; it radiates the belief of its maker.

Of course, my perspective is compromised, complicit. Is it simply too painful for me to relinquish his belief, to imagine that all of that effort was wasted? Or, to put a more positive spin on it, to accept that, for my father, the process was its own reward?

Or is there a type of art that only makes sense, a gesture that can only be completed, by the death of the artist?

> *The universe as a vast garbage heap of matter, a constant recycling of elements, an indifference to their use or purpose (the universe as a pile of junk).*
>
> —From my father's notebooks, 1995

My family moved to SoHo from the Lower East Side in 1968, when I was two. My father, Peter Pinchbeck, was an abstract artist who worked on an enormous scale, commensurate to his ambition. My mother, Joyce Johnson, was a book editor for the Dial Press and a novelist. SoHo was a failing commercial district of cheap lofts. We were part of the first wave of artists moving into the area.

During the day, trucks rattled down the crumbling paving stones of the old streets. Laborers yelled to each other as they hauled crates from the trucks onto the concrete landings. Walking with my parents, I would peek into the windows of small factories and watch steel cutters spinning, sending out sparks.

A rag trader worked out of our building. Louie was an Orthodox Jew with a long beard and pouches of wrinkles under his eyes. Giant bales of rags blocked up the lobby and the cavernous freight elevator. I never discovered who used these rags, or what they were for. I still wonder to this day. I hid from my parents inside the elevator, slipping behind the rag bales, which smelled of mildew and old dust—an oily, citrus smell. The elevator's iron gate crashed shut, and at our floor my father rolled up the massive door, which was too heavy for a child to budge.

At night, the streets fell silent. Time seemed to stop. Occasionally, an alley cat screeched, or the footsteps of a lone passerby echoed against the buildings. When I walked with my parents at night, the stillness pressed down on us. Ghosts seemed to hover above the old streets. It is bizarre to recall now, but SoHo in my childhood was marked by eerie emptiness.

The loft was an enormous cavern, a long rectangular box with eighteen-foot ceilings. Gridded windows at each end let in a dull gray light. In those days my father made large wooden constructions and painted colored rectangles that floated on vast sheets of stretched canvas. Most of the space was used for his studio. For my mother and me, he built bedrooms out of wooden beams and Sheetrock and installed bathroom fixtures and a water heater. But the living quarters were clearly provisional, an afterthought. My mother said the loft had once been a clothing factory. She showed me old needles she found between the rough floorboards.

When you are a child, everything belongs to a process that is both mysterious and essential. I didn't separate the work my father did on his paintings from the world of the streets, the rattling trucks and rag bales, the laborers and spinning machines. I assumed my father's paintings were necessary to the running of the entire system. I think I believed that most fathers spent their nights and days like he did, organizing colored shapes on enormous surfaces. To my child's mind, his constant activity seemed to have a vital connection to the city's mechanical processes. It was as if he was trying to distill some totemic essence from that confused tangle of trucks and streets and machines.

After my parents split up in 1971—their marriage destroyed by a lethal combination of the Sexual Revolution, Max's Kansas City, and my father's bad behavior—I would visit him every few weeks. He tore down the walls that created the illusion of a domestic interior to liberate the space. My bed was a small army cot set up in a corner of the studio, where I would sleep surrounded by his huge icons, breathing in the sweet and familiar odor of turpentine and oils.

Over time the neighborhood around us transformed, like a slowly developing photograph. The factories and loading platforms vanished one by one. Galleries and restaurants and boutiques appeared and proliferated, like new life forms escaped from some laboratory experiment. Once SoHo was declared chic, the rich descended on the area. They bought out the lofts that the artists vacated or were forced to leave. "The zombies," as my father called them. We still ran into my father's friends, with their paint-splattered jeans, their worn faces. But SoHo no longer belonged to them, and they were no longer comfortable in it. They had been outdated by the art stars and collectors who navigated the narrow streets in stretch limos, by the high-end boutiques that renovated the old tool and die shops. Range Rovers and Mercedes replaced the rattling trucks. Only the cast-iron buildings remained the same, like skeletons clad in new flesh.

Everything around him changed, but he remained constant, bunkered in his unrenovated loft, unwavering in solitary devotion to his art. As SoHo continued to transform, visiting him became increasingly like slipping behind enemy lines. His studio resembled the last hideaway, the last line of resistance in an occupied zone, and everything he brought forth—a bottle of brandy, a cigar—was like some object miraculously smuggled past the vigilant watch of the sentries.

His voice was like an old movie star's, deep and raspy, with a pronounced English accent. He had a full, ready laugh. Either he had a faint case of agoraphobia or a fear of revealing himself, as he liked to keep his jacket on, often wearing his sweater and coat even in overheated cafés. Possessed of a rare street-level social generosity, he was like an unappointed mayor of the old SoHo. He knew hundreds of people in the neighborhood, and he would often be late to meet me as he stopped to hail each person cheerfully, then listen to their sagas. His friend the painter Peter Stroud described him as "a true English eccentric."

In my twenties, when I passed through SoHo late at

night, after some party, I would detour by his block to see the light shining in his window. I would feel oddly secure in the thought that he was up in his loft, working, revolving like a planet through his self-created cosmology of painted shapes and plaster structures. He kept working in his loft until his death, of heart failure, in September 2000, at the age of sixty-eight.

> *the need to believe*
> —Handwritten note, found on my
> father's desk after his death

My father did not like to talk about his past; therefore, I know very little about it. I know that he was born December 9, 1931, in Brighton, a seaside resort on the southern coast of England. His father, Gerald Pinchbeck, an Irish Catholic pub keeper, left his mother when he was small, vanishing forever from his life. The Pinchbeck name adds its own twist to our story: We are rumored to descend from a line of celebrated English inventors and horologists. In the eighteenth century, Christopher Pinchbeck, an alchemist and clockmaker, invented pinchbeck, an alloy of tin and a type of false gold, as well as a mechanism to help people remember their dreams. In the nineteenth century, the word "pinchbeck" came to mean "anything false or spurious."

While he was growing up, my father and his mother often stayed with their relatives, collecting state assistance.

An early stint as an altar boy turned him against religion. Peter was trapped in London during the Blitz—he remembered emerging from the cellar after an air raid to see the house across the street blown to bits. He came of age during the bleak austerity of the postwar years.

"After the war, everything seemed gray. It was like all the color had been drained out of the world," he once told me. He saw an exhibit of van Gogh's paintings, then works by the Abstract Expressionists, at the Tate Gallery. Van Gogh's visions of rioting sunflowers and luminous night cafés inspired him to become an artist. He told me he wanted to put color back into the world. Lacking connections, he went to Paris, only to find that the School of Paris was dead. In the galleries, he saw shows of the New York School, and decided to move to New York.

He arrived in New York in 1960 to learn that the heyday of Abstract Expressionism had ended. He worked as an orange juice seller in the Fourteenth Street subway, then as a carpenter. He found a cheap loft on the rundown Bowery. In early photographs he looks intent, handsome, gaunt, his work shirts buttoned to the top button (he couldn't afford to heat his studio). His sculpture revealed the influence of the Russian Constructivists, his favorite art movement, as well as the Abstract Expressionists. He found a group of artists who shared his concerns, showing at Tenth Street galleries. He met my mother at a loft party in 1965. They married after she became pregnant.

During his life, my father failed to make a commercial

career out of his art. Most of his best exhibits came in the 1960s, when he was briefly associated with the Minimalists. In 1966, he showed wooden constructions in the *Primary Structures* exhibit at the Jewish Museum, curated by Kynaston McShine, which helped to launch Minimalism. "I suspect that Pinchbeck's work will shortly become known: it seems hard to believe that work of this authority and rectitude will go undiscovered for long," noted a critic in the magazine *Art International* in 1968. In 1971, his one-person show at the Paley & Lowe Gallery featured wooden boards of yellow, blue, and black, extending into space "with the equivalence of a gesture or perhaps a thought," wrote Carter Ratcliff in an *ARTnews* review. The exhibit appears in pictures to have been as beautiful as it was unsellable. After that, my father never had a stable relationship with a gallery.

During the 1970s, he turned away from sculpture and concentrated on painting. In a sense, he reverse-engineered art history, moving from Minimalism back to abstract painting that became increasingly gestural over the rest of his life. But even his most minimal objects had a hand-made touch, lacking the slickness of a Judd or a Morris. His signature works of the 1970s were paintings of squares and rectangles floating in colored fields. Despite his lack of a gallery—let alone any institutional support—he demonstrated a consistent and single-minded focus. He regularly painted works of outrageous size: fifteen feet or longer. The paintings were shown in some group shows and in

Barbara Rose's *Painting in the Eighties* (1979), at New York University's Grey Art Gallery. Most of them were never shown at all.

In the 1970s, large-scale non-ironic abstract paintings made by a straight man was the most unhip art imaginable. It was the era of Pop and Conceptualism, of political and feminist art. "Painting is dead" was a popular catchphrase. Pop and Conceptual artists used the distended macho ego and hand-wrought mysticism of the Abstract Expressionists as the punch line for their repetitive witticisms. Roy Lichtenstein, for example, Ben-Day-dotted a cartoon version of an AbEx brushstroke again and again. When Bruce Nauman made a neon spiral out of the phrase "The artist is the discoverer of mystical truths," it was obvious what movement he was mocking.

Unfortunately for his career, my father could not make concessions, strategize, or alter his work to fit a changing climate. For my father and a few of his friends, commitment to style was everything. Style was the mark of individual authenticity, of truth. If styles changed, leaving you outside the art world, you held onto your integrity. Like an old-time sea captain, you put your hand over your heart and you went down with the ship.

The art world boomed and busted and then moved to Chelsea. My father kept working in his loft. He moved from rigid rectangles to biomorphic squiggles, flying cigar shapes, shapes that smashed into and interpenetrated each other. He stacked old paintings against the walls. Sculptures made from cardboard, wood, and plaster curled around each other on the floor—bulbous columns and amoebic entities. Art supplies rested on long tables or the floor: power saws and staple guns, plaster and chicken wire, paint brushes sticking out of coffee cans, tubes of paint piled into cigar boxes. His living area consisted of a bed in a corner surrounded by paintings—little canvases of spinning shapes watching over him like spirit guardians—a large television set, and a desk overflowing with notes and papers and pill bottles. Next to his desk were two large sculptures, a blue column and a yellow zigzag made out of plaster. On his bulletin board, he pinned images and messages that inspired him, such as the Buddha's dictum "Everything is transient and nothing endures." Or from Cézanne: "You use pigment, but you paint with your feelings."

His last solo exhibit took place in 1989, and that was at a small space that lacked wall space to show his ambitious efforts, as well as the clout to get the work taken seriously by the art world. His work overpowered the venues in which he managed to show. The group exhibits he organized with his friends in banks and nonprofit spaces were, according to the art world's rigid hierarchies, almost worse than not showing at all.

My father never lost belief in art. He rarely lost his good cheer. Despite his lack of success, he knew he had achieved a lot. He had come to New York City alone, knowing no one, and with nothing to his name, and he had created himself. He preserved his vision, his integrity. Nobody could take that away from him.

He loved the physical act of painting, of brushing or scraping colored pigment on canvas. Painting infused his life with purpose. He streamlined his life so he could paint as much as possible. He eked out a living, teaching a day or two a week at Manhattan Community College, renting out part of the studio to a painter friend. Living in a huge loft in the wealthiest neighborhood in the world, he was always poor, his clothes baggy, his jackets smelling of mothballs. After his death, I looked at his IRS returns: Over the last decades, his annual income was usually under $10,000. When my father died, he had just a few thousand dollars to his name.

Today I remain amazed as well as shocked by his purity, his indomitable effort in the face of such total indifference.

"Only the rich will survive"
—Handwritten note, found on my
father's desk after his death

From time to time, over the course of many years, I tried without success to imagine one particular moment in my future. I tried to imagine the moment after my father's death, when I would enter his cavernous loft and confront forty years of his obstinate activity—his forceful bid for immortality—my bewildering patrimony. What would I do with it all? When I grasped toward this crisis, I quickly pulled back. I was left with a blank, a mental short-out like a blown fuse.

I never managed to discuss this with him when he was alive. It was often trapped in the back of my throat as we talked about other subjects. Even after he developed a heart condition, it seemed impossible for me to bring up this most serious and dangerous issue.

In the last few years of his life I also felt put off, even aggressed, by the titanic gesture, the seemingly pointless yet relentless activity of his incessant art making. I didn't enjoy visiting him as much as I did when I was younger. His loft felt increasingly claustrophobic, crowded with paintings and papers. I still recognized his gift—the authority of his line, his originality in color and composition. I still saw the power of the work (a few years ago, visiting him in his loft after an absence of some months, I was shocked at the sheer number of large, luminous paintings he had finished). But his effort seemed increasingly solipsistic, out of sync with the changing world. He seemed to be painting into the void. Struggling for my own survival in New York—not just a changed city, more like a different dimension of reality from the one my parents knew in the 1960s—I tried to distance myself from his doomed dedication.

Whenever I stopped to look at his paintings, I felt I was wearing a different lens on each eye—one brought the work too close, and the other left it too distant, so that the combined effect was a vertiginous loss of perspective. Useless as it was for me to believe it, I had always believed in his work. Inside his loft, his art had the eerie power of a fully realized obsession. It was an entire, self-constructed universe, a raw cosmology of forms and totems. He put everything he knew, everything he thought, every part of himself into it.

On the other hand, as a critic who wrote about contemporary art for magazines like *The Art Newspaper* and *Artforum*, I understood the forces that had condemned him to internal exile, to a death sentence inside an art world that rejected him. I knew why this type of painting was seen as hopelessly retrograde: It was too heartfelt, too expressive. It displayed no obvious novelty. I saw how the art system fed on new talent and youth—older artists who were not enshrined had to be pushed aside to make way for the next generations.

He never asked for my help, yet I felt helpless before the spectacle of his helplessness. I stopped writing about contemporary art for a few years, because I identified with his struggle, his belief. The burden was too heavy for me.

Sometimes I worried that his art had convoluted into a more private statement than it might have been, if he had found his place in the world. Sometimes the energy he put into the paintings—the brushstrokes pressing out from the canvas, the overwhelming color—suggested a willful transformation of negative experience into frantic and turbulent form. Ironically, in the time since his death, I find that the privacy, the obsessiveness, gives the work its power. I don't think I am wrong in recognizing that it also contains hints of wild, triumphant laughter.

It is strange: Now the entire weight of his unrecognized project has fallen directly on top of me, yet in some way I feel lighter, less crushed by that legacy than when he was alive. Before, I was paralyzed by it. Now that he is dead I am free to speak for his work as I would like. My father painted abstract forms that borrowed the expressive ambience of human beings; now, after his death, his work and his life become raw material I can arrange into text. I have become his interpreter as well as his curator. The situation provides an uncanny resolution to our Oedipal drama.

I am the inheritor not just of his paintings, but also of his vision, and of the desire to share that vision with the world.

> *As long as there is one beggar left in the world,*
> *there will still be myth.*
>
> —Walter Benjamin

After finding my father's body in his loft, after recovering from the first shock of grief, which is like a physical blow, then fighting through the city's nerve-wracking bureaucracy of death, which is its own special punishment of the living, after clearing out decades of accumulated junk and detritus, I began to spend a lot of time looking at his paintings.

It slowly dawned on me that he was a better artist than I had known. From his earliest sculpture to the last sketch, his work revealed an inner logic, a clarity of purpose, an emotional force that floored me. I started cataloging—an archaeological dig through the subterranean strata of his forty-year career, almost everything held within the same three-thousand-square-foot space.

I began to feel that I was learning through the paintings—not just about Peter Pinchbeck, but also about the nature of art itself, even something about writing. While the earlier geometrical paintings are rigidly ordered and flatly painted, his later works include passages that break out, scumbled and scratched surface areas that suggest cosmic chaos, night-lit abysses, fever dreams, the existential confinement of the self in its prison tower. They allow for awkwardness and grace, radiance and revelation, mystical hope as well as mute horror. They remind me of Henry Miller in books like *Black Sun*, riffing for pages on any subject—on a walk he took as a child, on a long-lost friend, or flourishing some metaphysical conceit. Miller's passages skate out toward the edge of collapse with seemingly careless abandon, then circle back to ensnare his meaning with precision. Scuffed, bohemian, almost abject yet oddly redemptive, my father's late paintings have that quality of a crisis confronted, a disaster averted—but just barely.

What he achieved toward the end of his life, I think, was a release based on those earlier decades of geometric constriction. His last decade was a revel in color and brushstroke, a brooding summation of his life-long inquiry. He exercised the freedom of someone who had dropped off the map—after one of his heart valves became infected a few years ago, he must have known that death was closing in on him, although he hid the truth of his condition from everyone, perhaps from himself as well. Escaping all fashions and trends, he gave up following anything except his own solitary path. In the paintings, he was whispering over and over that invisible secret he had carried with him all his life—from his early childhood in Brighton to the money-mad Manhattan where he had become an anachronism—that phantom of meaning and form that had haunted and pursued him. Working in solitude, over decades, he was proving the theorem to himself alone.

He was fascinated by physics and philosophy. He read constantly—Blanchot, Derrida, Wittgenstein, Nietzsche. Books on black holes and superstrings and chaos theory. Some of his late works could be seen as poetic images of quantum weirdness, molecular transformations, the space-curving force of gravitational fields. He was seeking some primal strata of shape and structure suggesting planets and atomic orbits, archaic tombs and menhirs, internal organs and essentialized bodies. Some of the work suggests a loony sexual subtext—two lumpy shapes sending a blur of fiery light between them in *Flashpoint* or in a late painting titled *Intimacy*, a gray rhizome-like form reaching a tubule out to probe its neighbor.

My father found contemporary art unbearable—I doubt he visited Chelsea more than two or three times. He loved the history of painting, spending many hours at exhibitions of Chardin, Bonnard, Cézanne, and so on. After his death, I found a scrawled note on his paint table describing his last work: "Painterly volume is what interests me. What shapes have to have is presence, like a person, have the reality of a figure in space, but still be abstract . . . I am influenced all the time by that Rembrandt self-portrait in the Frick where the figure sits against a dark background and the figure, face, and the amazing hands have an extraordinary volume and presence." At the end, he added: "Painting goes its own way. It must always evade our understanding."

After his death, it seems to me, the work has undergone a sea change. It is like a sponge absorbing his substance. In his absence, the art seems to expand and radiate. In some part of my mind I always suspected this could happen— somehow, his looming presence was an obstruction blocking his work from being seen or known, even by me. But why was this the case? After the decades of obscurity, had he given up hope in some way? Or did he always handle his career in a self-destructive manner? While cataloging, I have found no work from 1972 to 1977, the years after my mother left him, years when I rarely saw him. I imagine during that era bitterness overwhelmed him. He went down into the depths, passed through a psychic transformation. Afterward, he made his art for himself alone, with no regard for the outer world. Over the next decade, he slowly groped his way to a gestural style that expressed his personal and metaphysical concerns.

Despite his generous geniality, gallery people steered away from him. As time went on, something about him either failed to communicate or communicated too clearly—probably they caught the hint of wounded pride and maniacal seriousness underlying his cheerfulness, a dangerous taint in an industry increasingly devoted to fashion. I am sure they also intuited his disdain. In any case, older artists, especially those who have never been "hot," are not treated with kindness in the art world.

He was incompetent at presenting his work to those few people he met who might have helped his career. Since his death I have heard stories of well-meaning friends bringing collectors and dealers to the loft. He was barely able to clear wall space to show them a painting. He did not guide them through a progression of works, and they walked away baffled. When we talked about dealers and artists, he usually told stories of how this or that gallery had ripped off an artist in some way, hiding profits from them or letting work mysteriously disappear.

Perhaps he was ambivalent about living into the new century—in his notebooks he wrote about feeling that society was increasingly depersonalized, inhuman. He never owned a computer, never received an e-mail. In his notes he dreaded "the great Robot Empires of the twenty-first century." I think he felt that his belief system, the existential and handmade aura of his life and work, was not going to translate into this new era.

Death illuminates, clarifies the meaning of the life. While alive, the individual has only himself, a confusing mass of contradictory impulses and good and bad qualities. With death, he becomes a type, a representative of his age and time. During my father's life, his project seemed an impossible wilderness in which he was lost. With his death, the individual works fall into pattern, like musical notes unified in a symphony.

Sometimes I see the work he left behind as an elegy to painting itself—a farewell to the dream of heroic abstraction. And sometimes I think that no dream is ever lost.

> *A blade of grass, the suspended flight of a hummingbird. We are travelers in a land where signs elude us, and everything we think or do only magnifies our sense of loss.*
>
> —From my father's notebooks, 1995

But of course I could be totally wrong about his art. Sometimes I go back to the work and see only his effort, his volatile and at times unsteady struggle with paint. That struggle with primal materiality, in itself, is something we no longer see much in contemporary art. My father's struggle was particularly, peculiarly, naked. He is all there on the canvas—utterly defenseless, urgently himself.

There was something primordial, archaic, about him and his work, and he knew it. Paintings are named "Primordial Yearning," "Primal Longing." The work suggests the Freudian concept of the "oceanic," the unconscious impulse that seeks a merging of all dualities and opposites. The paintings compel the viewer's attention to swirl around the picture plane, following the surge of forces through the composition. In each painting, he tried to create tension and equivalence across the entire surface—absorbing a lesson from the "all-over" painting of the Abstract Expressionists. His paintings are not ironic, but the whirling, dovetailing shapes, the collapsed volumes, welcome a humorous response. He often chuckled as he showed them to me.

By his inability to deal with his career during his life, he left the question of the value of his work entirely open for me to define—as I always suspected he would. Now it is up to me to create a place for the work. Or I could let the work sink into the void, that vast garbage heap of all that is unknown and forgotten—that empty maw into which all celebrated enterprises eventually follow, albeit at a somewhat slower pace.

After death, could my father's helplessness and dedication be revealed as a kind of strategy—like Kafka or van Gogh, whose failures in life were redeemed by their work? As Emily Dickinson wrote in one of her little hand-stitched volumes, providing solace for generations of secret scribblers: "Publication is the auction of the mind of man." The artist's obstinate unworldly stance, so irksome and even intolerable while they stand before us, can be revealed as a willful negation, a hermetic "will to power." Their helplessness before life can become part of the story that establishes the work's integrity after death.

For a long time, my thoughts on his work would swing wildly between contradictory poles: "What are paintings on canvas except a metaphor for the light of the soul trapped inside the fading body?" I wrote in my journal soon after his death. I loved his work, hated the burden— but sometimes the polarities reversed and I found myself hating the work yet loving the burden. Attraction and repulsion is also a theme of the paintings, with shapes suspended in force fields of tension. He gave me the right to dumpster his gigantic efforts, give away the rest, choose a few small ones as mementos, get on with my life. I chose, instead, to hold onto his work, to await the possibility of a redemptive moment of posthumous recognition.

Sometimes I felt myself sucked toward the abyss of my father's project—his unrecognized gift and enormous drive, his helplessness, the paintings themselves like naked beings crying for attention (some of them even look strangely like radiant babies). After he died, I realized that somewhere in my mind I was always having a conversation with him about art, the meaning of art within society, the place of the artist, the value of the artist continuing his own work without a public. This conversation continued for many months after his death, finally dissipating, as life moved on.

I recognize a pinchbeck quality to this whole enterprise: However I present his work now, in his absence, is a bit of a lie—like all texts, this essay is itself full of errors, secret hedges, misperceptions recalibrated as fact. It is a deeply heartfelt yet spurious exercise. Some of our Pinchbeck ancestors in England were, apparently, alchemists, and I am aware that to make of my father's career something he failed to make in his life requires a kind of alchemy. It requires storytelling, and storytelling, like painting or the Great Work, is an attempt to transmute the raw and transient stuff of life into something precious and sustaining.

With this task, whatever I do, I become the father to my helpless father.

> *That life is loss, that you can only hold things together for a limited time, and that despite all your efforts everything falls apart.*
> —From my father's notebooks, 1996

My father once told me an anecdote about an important critic in the 1970s. The critic was curating an exhibition of large sculpture. She made an appointment to see a piece he had finished. But the time came, and she called to say she couldn't make it. She said she would reschedule the meeting, but she never did. My father was forced to put his sculpture out on the concrete landing. He called a garbage disposal to take it away. From his fire escape, he watched the men put the sculpture in the back of the truck. He saw the sculpture go down the street and out of his sight. His whole career was stories like that one, repeated ad infinitum: So many slights, so many stings.

He never had his moment. Through a profound internal process, he made all of the rejections fuel his belief. He continued to work, without compromise, for nearly forty years. I feel lucky that I seem to have inherited a bit of his willpower. Once—a few years before he died—I asked him if he would accept his situation again: If he could go back in time and alter his style, in exchange for exhibits and attention, would he do it?

No, he said. Looking back, he would change nothing.

In the end I think he was a happy man.

SPECIAL THANKS

I want to acknowledge the following individuals for their support, friendship, encouragement, and inspiration:

João Amorim, José Argüelles, Liz Brackbill, Stuart Braunstein, Michael Brownstein, Giancarlo Canavesio, Charles Eisenstein, Jeffrey Hagerman, Graham Hancock, Brandie Hardman, Herwig Maurer, Laura Hoffmann, Mitch Horowitz, Heather Hill, Harlan Emil Gruber, Alejandro Jodorowsky, Ron Johnson, Ken Jordan, Kathi Von Koerber, Lewis Kofsky, Amber Kusmenko, Speed Levitch, Chris Lindstrom, Eli Mishulovin, Jennifer Palmer, Jonathan Phillips, Paradox Pollack, Michael Robinson, and Sarabeth Stroller DeLeury Schalk.

Daniel Pinchbeck is the bestselling author of *2012: The Return of Quetzalcoatl* and *Breaking Open the Head: A Psychedelic Journey into the Heart of Contemporary Shamanism*. He is the coeditor of *Toward 2012: Perspectives on the Next Age*. His writing has appeared in *The New York Times Magazine*, *Esquire*, *Wired*, *The Village Voice*, *LA Weekly*, *ArtForum*, *Arthur*, and many other publications. He is the editorial director of Reality Sandwich and cofounder of Evolver (www.Evolver.net). He is featured in the documentary *2012: Time for Change*, directed by João Amorim and produced by Mangusta Films in conjunction with Curious Pictures.